Between Nostalgia and Apocalypse

DANIEL B. SHARP

Between Nostalgia and Apocalypse

POPULAR MUSIC AND

THE STAGING OF BRAZIL

WESLEYAN UNIVERSITY PRESS

Middletown, Connecticut

Wesleyan University Press
Middletown CT 06459
www.wesleyan.edu/wespress
© 2014 Daniel B. Sharp
All rights reserved
Manufactured in the United States of America
Typeset in Galliard by Integrated Publishing Solutions

Wesleyan University Press is a member of the Green Press Initiative.
The paper used in this book meets their minimum
requirement for recycled paper.

Library of Congress Cataloging-in-Publication Data
Sharp, Daniel B.
Between nostalgia and apocalypse: popular music and
the staging of Brazil / Daniel B. Sharp.
pages cm. — (Music culture)
Includes bibliographical references and index.
ISBN 978-0-8195-7501-2 (alk. paper) — ISBN 978-0-8195-7502-9
(alk. paper) — ISBN 978-0-8195-7503-6
1. Sambas — Brazil — Pernambuco — History and criticism. 2. Popular
music — Brazil — Pernambuco — History and criticism. 3. Popular music — Social
aspects — Brazil — Pernambuco — History. I. Title.
ML3487.B77P47 2014
781.640981 — dc23
2014018629

5 4 3 2 1

Contents

Introduction

In 1938, when Dona Senhorinha Freire Barbosa was eighteen years old, the Mission of Folkloric Research visited her hometown of Tacaratu, Pernambuco, as part of a trek through Northeast Brazil to record folk music. Recordings of Dona Senhorinha—informant 490—contributed to a project that profoundly shaped notions of Brazilian musical patrimony. The Mission of Folkloric Research, envisioned by the celebrated modernist writer and musicologist Mário de Andrade, recorded in several interior towns in the states of Pernambuco and Paraíba, including Tacaratu, Patos, Pombal, and Arcoverde, the epicenter of the research reported in this volume.

The team of recordists brought the discs from the rural interior of the Northeast to an archive in the more industrialized Southeast, where scholars and musicians defined Brazilian musical folklore as they compiled the tracks. Composers and performers treated the melodies from Mário de Andrade's expeditions as "raw materials," forging a new framework of musical Brazilian-ness and contributing to the rise of samba as a national emblem. The combination of Luso- and Afro-Brazilian musical sensibilities came to celebrate cultural and racial mixture as a source of Brazilian national uniqueness. Andrade's itineraries reinforced this particular musical mapping of culture. Within the story of samba, the Northeast serves a reservoir of tradition, while Rio de Janeiro in the Southeast serves as the site where the genre later coalesced.

The Brazilian ethnomusicologist Carlos Sandroni was pleased to find informant 490 still alive and well when his recording project retraced the route of the Mission of Folkloric Research sixty-five years later, in 2003. None of those who were recorded in 1938 had been granted access to the recordings, which had remained in São Paulo ever since the expedition returned there. His video camera rolling, Sandroni placed bulky headphones on the elderly woman's head. Her eyes lit up as she heard the recording of her voice for the first time. Dona Senhorinha became nostalgic as she listened to the song. She was delighted to recognize herself and began to sing along, reminiscing about another singer on the recording, whose voice she recognized. After the song finished playing she began to remember other songs from her childhood. She jumped up and, despite her frail frame, managed to demonstrate the *coco* dance step.

The showing of the video of Dona Senhorinha was part of a weeklong meeting I attended in 2003 that gathered members and friends of Associação Respeita Januário, a nonprofit organization that Sandroni founded to support traditional musicians in the region. Dona Senhorinha and others from Tacaratu were there to watch the video of her being reunited with the sound of her youthful voice. Their presence changed the emotional tenor of the event. The intellectual register of researchers' progress reports was eclipsed by the strong response from the Tacaratuenses upon hearing old melodies.

Dona Senhorinha's emotional response to the recordings was to be expected. She had moved from rural Tacaratu to the capital city of Recife and thus was remembering both the *place* where she used to live and the *era*. Rural-urban migration plays a part in painting a folkloric patina on rural areas and smaller, interior towns and cities. Thus, musical fieldworkers travel to the hinterlands, where they believe traditions still endure that have faded in more urban, industrialized areas. In Brazil, with its uneven economic development, recording projects such as the Mission of Folkloric Research have represented entire regions nostalgically as repositories of heritage and folklore.

The northeastern interior region in particular has suffered extreme poverty, drought, and massive outflows of rural-urban migration in search of economic opportunities on the coast and in the Southeast. The region has been represented in popular music, literature, and film not only as a nostalgic space, but also as a space of rebellion and millenarianism, where violent bandits are celebrated for their vigilantism and maverick Catholic mystics preach the apocalypse.

Brazilians use the word *saudade* to express the multiple registers of nostalgia: individual and collective, universal and uniquely Brazilian. *Saudade* is not simply a straightforward translation of the word "nostalgia," but rather an expression of a deep longing or sense of loss that has come to be conceived as a generalized affect of Brazilian-ness. The bittersweet yearning of *saudade*, described by Joaquim Nabuco as "remembrance, love, grief and longing" all at once, is often understood to be ever present in Brazilian life. The anthropologist Roberto da Matta evocatively describes *saudade* as "an enchanted temporality that contaminates" (1993, 34).

Cultural Rescue in Arcoverde, Pernambuco

After the screening of the video of Dona Senhorinha, researchers gave a presentation on musicians in Arcoverde, Pernambuco, a small commercial city on the edge of the desertlike *sertão* interior of the state. The poet, historian, and literary scholar Micheliny Verunschk and the ethnomusicologist Cristina Barbosa described how new notions of citizenship, heritage, and tourism were scraping against older notions of folklore.

Micheliny explained that when she grew up in Arcoverde in the 1980s, it was widely considered "a place without history, without memory, and without culture," a sentiment shared throughout Brazil during the fits and starts of redemocratization during the transition out of decades of military dictatorship. She expressed a desire to discover an Arcoverde where she would want to raise her own children someday. In what she described as an "active reconquest of identity," Micheliny learned about the history of *samba de coco* from Lula Calixto, a singer and street vendor widely known as a town eccentric. Micheliny described Lula as a link to an older generation of *samba de coco* musicians. He sold coconut candy on the streets of Arcoverde and offered to teach *samba de coco* to anyone who would stop and listen. He tirelessly sought out sympathetic teachers, who allowed him to teach in elementary schools. Lula considered this his calling.

Coco is a style of music and dance principally associated with poor Afro-Brazilians from the coastal Northeast, not the dry interior where Arcoverde is located.[1] It is mainly found in the state of Pernambuco and adjacent coastal states. *Coco* consists of layers of percussion with an asymmetrical 3 + 3 + 2 pulse *tresillo* timeline (counted ONE and two AND three and FOUR and). Backing vocals respond with short refrains, and songs alternate between verses and rapid-fire improvised, declamatory sections called *emboladas*, or tongue twisters. There are myriad variations on *coco*. One of the most prevalent styles in Pernambuco is *coco de embolada*, in which two dueling tambourine players trade insults, play word games, and provide social commentary on street corners and beaches.

The recognition of *coco* as music that harbored the essence of Brazilian-ness can be traced back to Mário de Andrade, who gushed about a *coco* singer named Chico Antonio whom the Mission recorded in 1929, claiming that Antonio's voice "managed to distill the quintessence of this way of ours of singing. It is a subtle nasal quality, good and sweet but with a strong bite to it, not unlike the bittersweet taste of the cashew fruit" (Andrade 1959, 378). Andrade's writings about Chico Antonio cemented *coco* as part of the key musical vocabulary used in modernist explorations of Brazilian-ness. The melodies and recordings that Andrade brought back to São Paulo provided composers with the ingredients to "rediscover" Brazil musically.

Samba de coco, the specific variety of *coco* played in Arcoverde, is one of many Afro-Brazilian round dances commonly understood to have preceded samba, such as *samba de roda* in the state of Bahia, *jongo* from the state of Rio de Janeiro, and *tambor de crioula* from the state of Maranhão. The genre indexes both the more Afro-Brazilian coastal Northeast and the white and *mestiço* arid *sertão* backlands. Its repertoire overlaps with the accordion-driven *forró* dance music emblematic of the northeastern interior. In contrast to coastal *coco*, *samba de coco* in interior Pernambuco also varies in terms of instrumentation: the triangle and a small *surdo* bass drum are included, and large *bombo* drums are not, yet the *ganzá* shaker and *pandeiro* are present in both styles.

In her speech at the meeting Micheliny revealed that the street musician Lula Calixto had died in 1999 of Chagas disease, shortly after she finished her research with him on *samba de coco*. There is a direct connection between Chagas disease and poverty: the beetle that transmits the disease lives in thatched houses made of mud, but not in the sturdier and higher-cost, tile-roofed brick or cinder block houses. It is an ironic and tragic twist that a quaint, folkloric mud hut replica later served as a museum in his honor.

Micheliny noted that only after Lula's death and the media attention surrounding it did the city formally recognize *samba de coco*. It has since become the "sonic postcard" of Arcoverde that promotes the city to tourists. As one of the attractions drawing tourists to visit, Lula Calixto's family built a bar in the front part of their house and a small museum across the street. In the bar family members receive visitors and hold impromptu "rehearsals" at which the family group sings songs and encourages everyone present to dance *coco*. In the museum visitors are invited to learn the story of the group through an exhibition of photographs and Lula's personal effects.

The next day, three members of Lula Calixto's family, Assis, Iuma and Iram, stood on the auditorium stage and answered questions about the group that Lula founded: Samba de Coco Raízes de Arcoverde (Samba de Coco Roots of Arcoverde), or simply Coco Raízes. Assis, a stout, soft-spoken carpenter around sixty years old with a striking mixture of indigenous and Afro-Brazilian features, fielded questions in a clipped *sertão* accent. He had never written a song before his brother Lula passed away four years earlier. But after Lula was gone, Assis felt compelled to carry on his brother's dream of sustaining a *samba de coco* group and began to write lyrics and invent melodies. Assis's slender, beautiful niece Iuma demonstrated the two steps of *samba de coco*—the quick *trupé* and the slower *parcela*—as Assis clapped a *tresillo* rhythm and tentatively sang one of his compositions in this formal setting. As Assis sang lead, Iram and Iuma responded with insistent refrains in ringing vocal harmony.

Coco Raízes was not the only band in Arcoverde that had achieved popular and commercial success. When Micheliny Verunschk conducted her research on the history of popular music and culture in the city, she was helped by her friend José Paes de Lira Filho, known as Lirinha. As Micheliny recorded interviews, Lirinha learned songs and *pandeiro* tambourine techniques. After they finished their research, Micheliny wrote a report, and Lirinha started a band called Cordel do Fogo Encantado, playing music inspired by the styles he had learned. Lirinha wrote and sang about the Alto do Cruzeiro neighborhood where the much of the Calixto family lived, several blocks uphill from Lirinha's family home. A large, white, cement cross stands there at the top of the hill; it is a scenic point removed from and overlooking the town's center. Walking up the hill to the Alto do Cruzeiro became pivotal to Lirinha's artistic development. It was where he heard the source of his inspiration and where his musical apprenticeship took place.

Before the weeklong meeting I had only heard of Arcoverde at a concert by Cordel, as the group calls itself.[2] The iconoclastic pop band was influenced as much by radical, experimental theater as by local folklore. It was led by Lirinha, who sought through its performances to reappraise past cinematic and literary representations of the region as a territory of poverty, violence, and drought. Cordel's performances were a stormy, apocalyptic experience that evoked the cinematic, mythical northeastern *sertão* of violent bandits and millenarian maverick Catholic preachers. The band combined the incantatory tone of fire and brimstone prophecy with hypnotic, percussion-heavy Afro-Brazilian sacred music. Cordel feverishly bent music marked as regional and traditional, such as *samba de coco* and *reisado*, so that its performances would stand up to the strident intensity and volume of a heavy metal or punk rock show. At nearly every performance the group claimed *samba de coco* as one of its main musical influences.

From a very young age Lirinha had been reciting popular poetry at state-sponsored contests in the *sertão* interior. Over time he had honed a very particular rural Pernambucan accent, and his vocal style was declamatory, occupying a space between speech and song. What began as a folklore revue eventually morphed into a visceral, screaming onslaught. Cordel became known all over Brazil in mostly college-educated and left-intellectual circles that listened to alternative commercial music released on independent recording labels. The band was lauded by critics, and its presence nationwide was growing as band members appeared on Brazilian MTV and in *sertão*-centered films (*Deus é Brasileiro, Árido Movie*). To fans and critics in Recife Cordel represented the second generation of *mangue beat*, a Recife-based music scene featuring a rooted cosmopolitan sound that bridged youth music and national music in the early to mid-1990s (Avelar and Dunn 2011; Galinsky 2002; Sharp 2001; Teles 1998, 2000).

Mangue beat recombined local or regional Afro-diasporic styles such as

Afro-Pernambucan *maracatu* and *coco* with global pop staples such as hip-hop and punk rock. Short-lived but influential, *mangue beat* distanced itself from previous regionally identified musics; musicians such as Chico Science described their sounds as *envenenado* or poisoned, to express their disdain for traditional purism. The moves to embrace and recombine "foreign" and "local" genres within *mangue beat* were jarring for many in the early 1990s, since much of youth culture had maintained more of a separation between national and international styles during the 1980s. After Chico Science, the lead singer of the seminal *mangue beat* band Chico Science e a Nação Zumbi, died in 1997, Lirinha was widely considered the most charismatic front man from Pernambuco. Although Cordel purposely distanced itself from the *mangue* label, claiming its *sertão* heritage to be distinct from developments emerging from the mangrove swamps of coastal Recife, its fan base overlapped considerably with *mangue* pioneers Chico Science and Mundo Livre S/A. As Cordel's career momentum began to build, the band moved its headquarters first to Recife and then to São Paulo and launched national and international tours.

For all Cordel's disruptive fury, the band can be seen as carrying on a tradition. Lirinha is an important recent figure in the history of Música Popular Brasileira (MPB), because Cordel can be considered part of a lineage of "anthropophagic" popular music that dates back to *tropicalismo*, a late 1960s movement that sought to move away from stiff notions of Brazilian musical nationalism. *Tropicalistas* such as Caetano Veloso and Gilberto Gil from nearby Bahia rejected the easy coupling of particular musical styles with particular regions. Instead, they proposed that the ability to culturally "cannibalize," or critically assimilate and cobble together, cultural inflows was central to the national character. The *tropicalistas* drew from the revolutionary avant-garde in cinema, art music, poetry, and art, as well as an array of Brazilian, Latin American, and global pop styles. They juxtaposed images of affluence and poverty, folklore and commercial pop, and experimentalism and traditionalism to create an absurdist portrait of the nation.

Lirinha's apocalyptic, prophetic affect stands in stark contrast to the pointed but often playful Dadaism of *tropicalismo*. Nevertheless, both are concerned with the origins of Brazilian-ness and how these origins inform the present. This concern sets them apart from the majority of groups in Brazil's increasingly genre-differentiated music industry, where recent ambitious attempts to sum up Brazil through popular music are relatively few and far between.

During the Associação Respeita Januário meeting, the term *resgate*— literally translatable as "cultural rescue"—surfaced several times as a point of contention in descriptions of *samba de coco*. The efforts of Micheliny and Lirinha, and subsequently of the public and semiprivate institutions Fundarpe (Pernambucan Arts Foundation), SESC (Social Service of Commerce), and Petrobras (the Brazilian national oil company), had led many to use the word. Yet Micheliny and Lirinha, as well as many others, felt uneasy about the process of cultural rescue. Some speakers expressed misgivings that *cultural rescue* implied that melodies *must* be documented because they were on the cusp of vanishing. Other members countered that there was indeed an urgency to their efforts to register traditional music before it was eclipsed by television, Internet, and shopping mall consumerism. It seemed unclear to those present at the meeting, myself included, how to proceed with studies of folklore without falling into what Tobing Rony calls the "taxidermic" mode of ethnographic representation, which makes "the dead look alive, and the living look dead" (Rony 1996, 126). Critiques like Tobing Rony's are present when Brazilian scholars and musicians accuse those they consider purists of placing a culture in formaldehyde and denying its constant transformation as a dynamic, mutating form. One particularly memorable phrasing of this criticism was by the Brazilian anthropologist Hermano Vianna, who once argued that "rescue is what you do for kidnapped people, or people who have accidents," not for musical genres (Gasperin 2000).

I believe that the misgivings expressed at the meeting can be understood, at least in part, as unease about the nostalgia that *resgate* arguably represents—what Svetlana Boym refers to as "restorative nostalgia" (2001). Boym splits "longing for home" into halves: *restorative* nostalgia and *reflective* nostalgia. Restorative nostalgia tells a story of returning to one's origins and is tied to attempts to reconstruct a phantom home. A celebratory notion of homeland that disavows the shame and embarrassment lurking in a nation's past is an example of restorative nostalgia.

Reflective nostalgia, on the other hand, is more ambivalent and many-plotted. It is more concerned with fragments and ruins than with unity and wholeness. The themes of migration and exile are central, and the contradictions of modernity are acknowledged and explored. Reflective nostalgia is constituted by, not opposed to, uprootedness and diaspora. Whereas restorative nostalgia touts itself as truth and tradition, reflective nostalgia acknowledges itself as longing and clears a space for doubt. As Boym phrases it, reflective nostalgic can be "at once homesick and sick of home" (2001, xix).

I find Boym's typology useful to interpret the respective efforts of musicians from Arcoverde, even though both Coco Raízes and Cordel restlessly inhabit and unsettle both nostalgias. For example, members of Cordel speak about Arcoverde as their hometown and the source of their inspiration during every performance. However, the Arcoverde they portray in their lyrics is not an idealized hometown. Instead, it is a stormy, gothic place in which a hunger riot overtakes a supermarket, and a bitter clown, his makeup smeared like blood, performs in a desperate, threadbare traveling circus on the outskirts of town.

In Arcoverde I find the two categories of nostalgia difficult, if not impossible, to pry apart. Arcoverde offers an excellent case in point of how mutually constituting these categories of nostalgia are. Over the course of this book I explore how Cordel straddled the restorative and the reflective, charting how it became entangled in a restorative project before moving toward a reflective approach to performance. I examine how its success as an "antirestorative" band nevertheless bolstered restoration by attracting fans to visit the group's hometown. I detail the circumstances in which Cordel's project strives to appear restorative only from a distance, so that it won't fall from the good graces of certain sponsors.

On first glance Coco Raízes and other *samba de coco* performers work within the restorative mode. Closer scrutiny, however, raises questions regarding their status as well: How is a restorative project unsettled when musicians from previously excluded groups such as Afro-Brazilians seek social recognition through claims to local tradition that reiterate nostalgic narratives? The story told by *samba de coco* during the São João Festival is a ready-made tale of rural homecoming. It is restorative and government-friendly, pitched in a register of premodern innocence. Yet what distinguishes it is that these particular Afro-Brazilian storytellers most likely wouldn't have had a space to tell it in the *sertão* only decades before.

Popular Music and Citizenship

Lula Calixto once said that being valued as an artist made him feel like a citizen. He was pointing out that music was a means for him to become socially audible within his city and in Brazil as a whole. Lula made this comment in the late 1990s, at a moment of redemocratization and the expansion of citizenship in Brazil following more than two decades of military dictatorship. It was also during this time that the particular nostalgias evoked by Coco Raízes and Cordel performances began to resonate with a broader public. Popular music in Brazil is located at the center of these new tensions, just as it was located at the center of older narratives of racial and cultural mixture, civility, and nationalism that make up the durable samba paradigm. Social inequality persists in the postdictatorship period, but ideologies of universal inclusion, such as the notion of racial democracy, no longer succeed in blurring this inequality. For many insurgent citizens, racial democracy, carnaval, and samba have become tainted by a veneer of easy civility and accommodation to extreme social inequality, an acceptance of racial and class ambiguity that undermines taking a stand in defense of one's rights.

This questioning of civility (and the rhetoric of the "cordial Brazilian") is being worked out through music. As samba remains entangled with the universalist rhetoric of racial democracy, alternatives such as rap, funk, rock, and heavy metal have flourished in Brazil since the 1980s. These more aggressive musical aesthetics have come to represent an opting-out of the samba paradigm in favor of more polarized views of race, social class, and Brazilian-ness. By the mid- to late 1990s, when Cordel and Coco Raízes emerged, an impulse to reassess "deep, authentic" Brazil followed in the wake of democratization. Both bands can be seen as part of this continued reassessment of the samba paradigm, while at the same time insisting that this reworking can take place without needing to reject national and regional musical and poetic reserves outright in favor of global genres of popular music.

Many Brazilians in urban *favela* shantytowns and rural encampments practice what Holston (2008) terms "autoconstruction," meaning that they build their own shelter brick by brick as they can afford it. Meanwhile, urban elites and much of the middle class have moved into fortified high-rise buildings that "stigmatize, control, and exclude those who had just forced their recognition as citizens" (ibid., 281). The appeal to coastal festivalgoers of Arcoverde as a small-town getaway where they can dance *samba de coco* is located within this dynamic of shantytown autoconstruction and high-rise fortification. The friendly *favela light* of the Alto do Cruzeiro located in the *sertão light* of Arcoverde concretizes visitors' desire to return not only to an idealized rural point of origin, but also to an imagined moment of civility and easy socializing across racial and class lines that is perceived to have been lost in large cities in recent decades.

Coco Raízes occupy the older homecoming narrative of São João, playing music that, despite the "samba" in *samba de coco*, is more aggressively stomped than gracefully swung. The group pays tribute to the Landless Rural Workers' Movement (Movimento dos Trabalhadores Rurais Sem Terra, MST) in its lyrics, while performing a genre that embodies, through dance, autoconstruction—in that stomping was necessary, the story goes, to tamp the dirt floor down after the completion of a thatched-roof mud house. In the performances of Arcoverde's musicians, the small city has become not an escape from a cycle of autoconstruction and fortification, but rather a setting where the meanings of this dynamic are being worked out and stomped upon.

Intangible Heritage

In 2003 the United Nations Educational, Scientific and Cultural Organization (UNESCO) formulated a new category for preservation efforts called "intangible heritage." The performances of the particular *samba de coco* musicians in this book don't officially qualify as "intangible cultural heritage of humanity," although the designation was given to comparable musicians playing *samba de roda* in nearby Bahia. Nonetheless, the story of *samba de coco* plays out in the shadow of this reworking of cultural preservation on the level of global metacultural decision making. The development of the new category was one of many acts that contributed to the broader contemporary shift in how folklore and heritage are now understood.

Intangible heritage draws from previous efforts to protect tangible heritage and natural heritage. *Tangible* heritage is cultural and nonliving; *natural* heritage is natural and living. *Intangible* heritage is cultural, like a museum artifact, but unlike tangible heritage, it is living, like a forest. The remolding of folklore into intangible heritage has led to preservation efforts with a more holistic focus, not just on the "masterpiece," but on the "master" and his or her practices and surroundings. Yet this effort to move beyond the artifact and the museum and into the realm of protecting ephemeral cultural practices is proving to be a delicate business. It risks treating people as things to exhibit or as animals and tracts of land to conserve. Use of the terminology "carriers," "bearers," and "transmitters" of tradition risks implying that people thought to possess intangible heritage are passive vessels or objects rather than strategic actors in heritage productions (Kirshenblatt-Gimblett 2004, 58).

In this book I detail how actors in heritage productions adopt stances on and off the stage with the aim of asserting themselves as neither passive vessels nor objects. My aim is to scrape the folkloric patina off a Brazilian hinterland and examine the tangle of interests that strategically use the past, including institutions fueled by cultural nationalism, industries promoting tourism and entertainment, and the musicians themselves. This ethnographic case study begins around 1995, when musicians performing marginal-turned-traditional *samba de coco* gained increased access to festival stages and recording studios. Studio recordings have been turning musical practices into tangible goods ever since the advent of the phonograph. More recently, however, a tourist experience resembling the classic paradigm of ethnographic fieldwork has emerged as well. Enterprising musicians marked as culture bearers are dramatizing short-term encounters with weekend visitors. This experiential folkloric touristic production exposes the complications of preserving heritage as it creates opportunities for an outmoded genre of music to live again as a representation of itself (Kirshenblatt-Gimblett 1998, 7).

Contemporary musicians living on the route of the 1938 Mission of Folkloric Research found that performing within genres steeped in nostalgia limited how they were received by audiences, even as it provided them with professional opportunities. Whether presenting themselves as culture bearers performing folklore or as pop innovators experimenting with a rooted cosmopolitan sound, they faced similar challenges. On both sides of a dynamic folk-pop boundary, musicians in Arcoverde reworked tradition to combat being discursively distanced from the Brazilian "here and now." Genres of music, poetry, and theater overlapped within cultural fields, producing a sense of contemporary northeastern-ness. As Arcoverde's musicians sought broader audiences, they attempted to rewrite the often unspoken rules underlying particular genres, such as, in this case, *música de raiz* (roots music), *mangue beat* (Recife-based mutationist pop music), and the broader *música regional* (regional music). Sometimes this engagement with genre involved downplaying the intertextual gaps or discrepancies between particular performances and their antecedents, and at other times these gaps were emphasized or even exaggerated in the service of distinguishing groups from others considered generically related (Briggs and Bauman 1992, 151).

As the musicians professionalized, they faced an idiosyncratic play of social inclusion and social exclusion. Being placed on a pedestal as the symbolic essence of their region did not inevitably translate into the material power of cultural citizenship, in which political enfranchisement and the positive recognition of social difference are all of a piece. The musicians sustained efforts to *abrir um espaço* (open a space) for other, more nuanced stories of their region to compete with well-worn stories that erased modernity and cast performers in a mythic register. Yet despite their successes, as they reached audiences beyond their region the musicians continued to find themselves ensnared in and sometimes reproducing the very discourses of heritage and folklore they sought to transform. They worked toward broader recognition while fighting against being treated as "ghostly fetishes of culture loss" (Ivy 1995, 10–11), hovering between the center and the margins.

I see this book as part of a broader movement in the last decade away from polarized celebratory and anxious discourses surrounding music and globalization that were common around the turn of the millennium. I hope to contribute to the "finer-grained historical ethnographic approaches to global music circulation" (Stokes 2004, 48). This story chronicles the movement of *samba de coco* from local pastime to staged performance projected into national and international circuits. Throughout I focus on what happens when people and commodities move between disparate institutions for support as their music circulates beyond their hometown.

Nostalgia, in its multiple registers, remains pivotal here, as it animates these stubborn discourses of heritage and folklore that both ensnare and enable musicians. It coexists as both a personal, individual longing and a collective emotion with historical and political dimensions, as the example of Dona Senhorinha illustrates. While Dona Senhorinha's reminiscing was personal, the context of her reaction was entangled in cultural preservation efforts. Sandroni's fieldwork culminated in a two-CD set of new recordings, *Responde a Roda Outra Vez* (*Answering the Circle One More Time*), with extensive liner notes, whose publication was funded by the Brazilian national oil company Petrobras.

Note on Research Methods

Micheliny Verunschk once observed that it was often difficult for Coco Raízes to discern which visitors were there to adore them and which were there to write about them, learn their music, help them, or take advantage of them. I felt this when I arrived. Accustomed to daylong, weekend, or weeklong visits by journalists and fans, family members were not sure whether to treat me with the full hospitality that they reserved for short-term guests, as just another Arcoverdense, or somewhere in between. Much ethnomusicology strives to meet Hood's (1971) ideal of bimusicality, in which a scholar travels somewhere, finds a music teacher, and spends much of his or her time becoming fluent in local musical codes. In my fieldwork, however, asking for too much musical instruction could potentially damage my relationships with musicians. As a researcher I chose to adopt a posture closer to that of a tourist or a long-form journalist than to that of an apprenticing musician, because the complications of musical apprenticeships were part and parcel of my object of study.

In this setting, insisting on musical instruction would have resulted in the musicians' questioning my motives for learning their style. They freely gave *pandeiro* tips to visitors who were only going to be there for a few days. But since I was there for a year, I decided to frequent the Alto do Cruzeiro only to listen, dance, and talk, rather than make learning to play music a first priority. The same should be said about recording. Issues of intellectual property rights were fraught and bitterly contested in Arcoverde in 2004, as the feuding Calixto, Gomes, and Lopes families began to release recordings commercially. As they recorded, issues surrounding legal authorship, ownership, and royalties surfaced. Making field recordings at this time proved to be highly contested, both because the recording would be seen as an act of allegiance to one family over another and also because many of the songs one group would record could be claimed by the other family as belonging to them.

I ended up adopting a timed approach, in which certain activities that weren't possible when I arrived proved possible before I left. Although I didn't take formal lessons, I absorbed the melodies alongside other fans. Near the end of my research year I occasionally played songs informally with Ciço Gomes, and he was patient with my attempts to sing harmonies with him. In 2004 I was among the first generation of ethnomusicologists to be able to bring along a laptop-based studio-in-a-backpack that could record multiple tracks simultaneously. Yet all of my close readings of songs by Cordel and Coco Raízes in this book are based on audio and video recordings made by others, not my own. I was excited by the prospect of actively producing multitrack recordings with musicians, following their vision and including their input during mixdown. And I was able to do this after living there four months, but only with musicians who maintained some distance from the feud and therefore ended up less central to this book. I was able to record Reisado das Caraíbas as group members sang their songs and recounted their histories; two cowboy singers, who even recorded a stylized *forró* CD with me; and Helton Moura and Alberone Padilha, who spent two months in my apartment-turned-studio, recording demo CDs that they then used to launch their careers. The only musical recordings of the Calixto women that I made feature them as guest backup singers on Alberone's songs.

An Ethnographer among Many

Conducting research in Pernambuco, I entered a field of collaboration and contestation. At Sandroni's meeting, scholarly and artistic experts were engaging in an ongoing conversation about folklore and heritage, grounded in a long history that traces back at least to Mário de Andrade and Luís da Câmara Cascudo in the pre–World War II era. I conducted my fieldwork in Brazil during the emergence of a tourist experience dramatizing fieldwork. The broader arc of this book tacks between the cultural and the metacultural—between cultural practice and cultural management. I also alternate between the musical and the ostensibly extramusical, including museum exhibitions, television documentaries, and buildings made of mud, which all contribute to efforts to anchor a particular location as a heritage destination. My goal is to chart the twists and turns of a mutating, contemporary notion of folklore and examine how these mutations affect the everyday lives of musicians from a canonized periphery. I focus on performances of heritage within the current moment, aiming to treat folklore in a way compatible with what Rabinow and colleagues term an "anthropology of the contemporary" (2008).

Between Nostalgia and Apocalypse is an ethnography of both the expert and the ordinary, without claiming that the boundary between the two is easily distinguishable in a scenario wherein knowledge is being produced by academics, journalists, performers, and tourists. I proceed in conversation with other ethnographers, such as Carlos Sandroni, Micheliny Verunschk, and Cristina Barbosa. Beyond simply engaging with my professional colleagues, however, I came to see many of the performers with whom I worked as conducting an ethnography-like endeavor in their own right as well. In saying this, I am aware that Lirinha will most likely bristle at this accusation. To him ethnography implies a kind of cold, intellectual process that he contrasts with his warm friendships and informal apprenticeships with older poets and musicians.[3] However, whatever he calls his process of gathering stories, poems, and melodies, it overlaps with Micheliny's process and my own. In addition, culture bearers and cultural entrepreneurs Iram and Assis Calixto and Severina and Leni Lopes, who erected competing museums exhibiting their versions of the story of *samba de coco* in Arcoverde, are also identifiable as ethnographers, as they display artifacts and shape discourses.

As one of many observers, I work from the position of the situated and partial ethnographer complicit within a field proliferating with ethnographers; performers conducting ethnography-like knowledge production; and visitors gathering words, images, and sounds as souvenirs and newspaper copy. As an ethnographer I aim to imbue performances, festivals, and moments from everyday life with a sense of proximity and vivid detail as I move between these various registers. I am not immune to the seductiveness of a nostalgic gaze toward a past that never was. My writing sometimes dips into a nostalgic mode, even as I seek to expose the ramifications of nostalgia used to further nationalist and commercial ends.

But where there is nostalgia, there is also a sense that the present is somehow unraveling. That is to say, the nostalgic mode is not my only companion here; echoes of a turbulent, apocalyptic mode periodically erupt as well. It is within the apocalyptic mode that Lirinha whips his audience into a frenzy with foreboding talk of the end of the world, or that a bitter feud between families of musicians underscores the volatility of being received as heritage. When family members slice their estranged relatives out of old photographs with razor blades or use microphones to shout bitter accusations rather than to entertain, they do so with a violent intensity that tears the picture postcard of nostalgia.

The first half of this book begins in the 1990s, tracing the emergence of *samba de coco* in Arcoverde as an emblematic cultural tradition and the rise of Cordel do Fogo Encantado as mutationist pop performers drawing tourists to the city. It chronicles the moment in which public and private initiatives enshrined rural musical practices as heritage and marketed them as popular culture.

Chapter 1 illustrates the provincializing process that *samba de coco* underwent as a genre, as musicians in Arcoverde accrued sponsors and began to perform as heritage. I explore how a markedly Afro-Brazilian musical form became an unlikely emblem of a city within the predominantly white and *mestiço* interior backlands. I also establish Cordel's initial posture of homage, which imbued the project with restorative nostalgia, a mode in which the musicians would later lose faith.

Chapter 2 explores the two museums that opened following a feud between two *samba de coco* families. I chart how the rise of *samba de coco* as a municipal emblem led to competing exhibitions of tradition. I outline how the Calixto and Lopes families documented their claims to the increasingly lucrative crown of local tradition. Focusing on the artifacts displayed and stories told in the two museums, I explore how the *samba de coco* families used homemade museum displays to make themselves visible (and audible) within the public sphere.

Chapter 3 explores the career trajectories of Coco Raízes and Cordel during the 2000s. Coco Raízes staged and choreographed *samba de coco* as the group became incorporated into Arcoverde's São João Festival and participated in circuits of regional roots music performance. Cordel in contrast, distanced itself from other regional, traditional groups as it shifted between genres, sponsors, venues, and audiences. As the band members questioned notions of folkloric tradition, they experimented with embodying on stage the bandits and millenarian figures who loom large in the history of the region. Eschewing sanitized, reassuring celebrations of place and tradition, Cordel deployed visceral Artaudian screams and Brechtian alienation effects to evoke a history of violence, drought, and hunger.

Chapter 4 explores how Cordel and the *samba de coco* musicians both inhabit and unsettle nostalgic modes of representation by examining the production of a television documentary about *samba de coco* and the MTV video produced by Cordel. I accompany the filming of a television documentary by TV Globo and interpret how editorial choices excised modernity from its depiction of Arcoverde, distancing musicians from the Brazilian here-and-now. In the MTV video, members of Cordel make the claim that both their roots in Arcoverde and their present longing for their hometown from afar are equally central to who they are, acknowledging the weight of tradition while justifying their move away from Arcoverde.

The second half of the book is an ethnography of the events that followed the entrance of *samba de coco* into the circuits of state sponsorship and the music industry. I focus on the São João Festival, as well as year-round tourism, to render a portrait of Arcoverde as a canonized periphery where contemporary struggles over citizenship and social inclusion play out through musical performance.

Chapter 5 centers on the 2004 São João Festival. It explores how the layout of the festival places musicians performing as heritage within developmentalist narratives of progress. I show how the hierarchical arrangement of stages displays a movement from primitive to modern, from past to present. I outline the range of performances that took place on these stages, some festooned with palm fronds and others outfitted with state-of-the-art sound and lighting systems. The multiple roles that musicians play as star performers, party hosts, souvenir craftspeople, bartenders, and waitstaff reveal the complexity of their position as entrepreneurial culture bearers.

The ambiguous status of *samba de coco* musicians is also a theme in chapter 6, in which I focus on new forms of cultural tourism. Encounters with visitors attracted to Arcoverde as a cultural tourist destination play out with a push and pull of intimacy and social distance. Visitors are encouraged to dance *samba de coco*, as long as they can't do it as well as the professionals. At an upscale folklore-themed restaurant, crêpes are named after local musicians. Staged "rehearsals" with visitors blur the line between outsider and insider. A *samba de coco* musician's dream of building a mud house replica of his childhood home as a tourist destination unravels when he returns to the rural site for the first time in a half century.

Chapter 7 is an elegy chronicling the dissolution of Cordel and the splintering of Coco Raízes as the 2000s came to a close. Based on follow-up ethnographic research undertaken periodically between 2005 and 2013, it charts the role of Arcoverde within a changing Brazilian cultural landscape during the presidency of Lula da Silva, a Pernambucan who grew up just down the road in Garanhuns. I detail changes in the São João Festival, examine Cordel's spectacular performance at the opening ceremonies of the 2007 Pan American Games, and describe the expansion of *samba de coco* tourist infrastructure as government funds sponsor the transformation of the Calixto house into a cultural center.

In the epilogue, I argue that the story of Arcoverde allows us to listen carefully to a postauthoritarian moment. It chronicles how redemocratization and the expansion of citizenship coexist in tension with neoliberal efforts to profit from tourist destinations. Both traditionalist and mutationist musical groups in Arcoverde have been reassessing the Brazilian national question during a moment of cultural reckoning. And neither those supposedly being "rescued" nor those doing the "rescuing" feel comfortable with their roles in this heritage drama. Instead, both are reaching beyond this older script and into new territory, where what it means to be Brazilian is being explored.

PART I

CHAPTER ONE

Staging Tradition

A week after the Associação Respeita Januário meeting, I drove to Arcoverde. The BR-232 highway running from Recife to Arcoverde had been recently repaved. Its lanes were doubled, reducing travel time to Caruaru, a city located 120 km from the capital. Billboards along the road advertised musical traditions to tourists. Caruaru, the largest city along the route, is a popular destination for the Saint John's Day celebration in June known as São João. It is touted as one of the largest, oldest São João celebrations in the Northeast. Every year festival events such as *quadrilha* line dancing in colonial garb are televised throughout the region. Caruaru also promotes pipe-and-tabor groups called *bandas de pífanos* and a large craft market at which musicians roam the aisles of vendors. Stalls display rows of miniature clay figures of accordion and flute players and the legendary bandit Lampião, a figure as notorious as Pancho Villa or Jesse James. Satirical miniature doctor/patient scenes are also popular. One scene features a tiny dentist placing his foot on the chest of a patient for better leverage, and another depicts the delivery of a baby. The figures represent an attempt, through caricature, to contain anxieties about health that are pervasive in a zone of harsh economic disparity.

Beyond Caruaru, the landscape became dotted with cacti and *caatinga* scrub brush. The BR-232 narrowed from two lanes each way to one each way, pockmarked with deep, harrowing potholes. Driving became more treacherous, as drivers boldly threatened oncoming traffic trying to pass each other. Several towns along the road promoted themselves as part of the Route of *Forró*, an effort to alert visitors to dance halls and small-town festivals. *Forró* is a genre label that encompasses several rhythmic variations on dance music and most commonly features accordion as its emblematic instrument. In its various subgenres, including ultrapopular *forró estilizado* and its more rustic counterpart *forró pé-de-serra*, it has crystallized as a regional genre promoted as the essence of the white and *mestiço* Catholic cowboy of the northeastern interior backlands. One aspect of the projected image of Arcoverde that sets it apart from the rest of the Route of *Forró* is the decision by its municipal government around 2000 to promote sounds strongly associated with coastal Afro-Brazilian-ness in the *mestiço* backlands.

As I drove through the crest of hills dividing the coast and the interior, I thought of a passage I had read about shrinking driving times, modernity, and change in the northeastern *sertão*. The passage had come from a seminal text on the *sertão* called *Vaqueiros e Cantadores (Cowboys and Troubadours)* by folklorist Luís da Câmara Cascudo. The book was written in December 1937, a few months before the Mission of Folkloric Research recorded in Arcoverde. I looked up the quotation later, so I could remember the excerpts that bridged the era of the Mission of Folkloric Research and that of Sandroni's recording project.

Câmara Cascudo's text betrays an ambivalence toward the passage of time, longing for a past way of life. Wonder, awe, and panic accompany the arrival of modernity in Cascudo's telling: "I lived in the typical *sertão*, that has now disappeared. Electric lights hadn't yet appeared. The gramophone dazzled us. Old João de Holanda . . . got down on his knees in the middle of the road and confessed all of his sins, blubbering, when he glimpsed, at sunset, his first automobile" (Cascudo 2004, 11).[1]

In contrast to the city and its ever-novel contraptions, Cascudo idealizes the distant past of his childhood in the *sertão*. In a key phrase he depicts it as unchanging, arguing that its past was whole in its present, unlike our present, in which the past is fractured and slipping from our grasp. Notice the entanglement of home, past, and childhood, pitched in a register of innocence: "The cooking remained loyal to the eighteenth century. Clothing reminded one of a museum retrospective. The strong prayers, the social habits, the traditional festivals, the way people talked, the superstitions, everything was the inescapable Past, complete, in the present" (ibid.).

Cascudo chronicles the drastically shrinking travel times to and from the *sertão* as vehicles and roads developed. He takes these dizzying changes as emblematic of broader cultural shifts in the area: "The transformation is subtle and daily. The roadways brought the *sertão* together with the *agreste*. Canceling out the distance, they mixed the environments. Today electrical lights, cars, radio, cold drinks, cinema, newspapers are everywhere . . . everything is close, due to the car. . . . From Natal to Caicó it used to take six days. Now the trip takes five hours" (ibid.).

At the time, when I was driving to Arcoverde, I recalled only his reflections on travel times. The passage that followed, however, complicated Cascudo's reflection on the acceleration of modern life in the *sertão*. He claimed that nostalgia was not much of an issue for those who lived in the *sertão*, arguing that they constantly picked and chose the aspects of modernity that they wanted to participate in and those they wanted to reject: "The *sertão* modifies itself quickly. It becomes more uniform, it becomes more banal. Naturally, this criticism doesn't work for those who live there. Modernized life is better than the old way of going by horse buggy and having to stop and rest all the time. Relatives of mine that refused to eat salads made with lettuce ("You think I'm a leaf-eating lizard, do you?") conduct business in São Paulo, coming and going by plane" (ibid.). Concluding the passage, he opposes modernity to tradition and praises holdouts who scorn these changes. Troubadours, according to Cascudo, are quixotic bearers of tradition whose audiences remain stubbornly loyal: "The *cantador* recoils in front of the Radiola, the Victrola, cinema, the illustrated magazine. But he conserves his audience. Restricted, limited, poor but steadfast in their admiration. The *cantadores sertanejos* still live" (ibid.)

Recording and broadcasting technologies, transportation, and highway infrastructure have intensified the circulation of people, sounds, and money in the arid backlands. The folkloric paradigm that Cascudo helped crystallize has given way to a new period of heritage tourism and commercial pop mutations. Yet certain narratives of folklore have proven durable in the face of new shifts, as tourism emerges that resembles a recording expedition in miniature. The desire to return to the premodern is a recurring and very modern trope, as is the impulse to celebrate the stubborn holdout like the *cantador*. When I arrived in Arcoverde, sixty-five years after Cascudo wrote *Cowboys and Troubadours*, I found that Cascudo's formulation of folklore often served as the script that musicians and audiences used to describe the musical practices performed there.

Arcoverde is nestled in a valley, increasing its rainfall and making it often greener than the semiarid *sertão* located only a few kilometers farther down the BR-232. As I entered the city, stiltwalkers in street clothes practiced their skills along the side of the highway.

I found a hotel amid downtown storefronts. A nearby ice cream parlor proudly displayed photos of employees posing with Globo television network stars who had recently stayed in Arcoverde while filming a desert-themed prime-time series. A specific kind of cosmopolitan hinterland, Arcoverde is a preferred location for filming footage in a *sertão* setting, without the actors having to sacrifice too many amenities.

In contrast to how television and film depict the location as a land of tradition and heritage, the home of *samba de coco* was firmly anchored in a modern, consumerist present. Three-story buildings with ceramic tile façades lined either side of the street. Shoppers were shielded from the blistering sun by overhanging second-story apartments. Young children and teenagers sat in Internet cafes open to the street, their eyes glued to computer screens. Stores displayed DVD players, digital cameras, clothes, shampoo, bicycles, televisions, fabric, and guitars.

The sheer number of stores seemed unlikely. Demand appeared disproportionately large, considering the city's population. It turned out that this district supplied consumer goods to residents of several nearby small towns and rural areas as well as Arcoverde proper. Compared to nearby cities, Arcoverde felt young, commercial, and modern. The city was located in one of the first regions of Brazil to be colonized five centuries before, yet even the oldest Catholic church was less than one hundred years old. Houses and apartment buildings for the middle and upper classes featured clean lines, flat roofs, and a minimum of ornamentation. Downtown was not overly crowded, but it had a bustle to it that contrasted with the slower pace evident in neighboring Buique or Pedra. The sidewalks were half full of people with places to go, parking spaces were not always easy to find, and stores did a brisk business. Were it not for the long lines of people waiting to receive meager government assistance checks, as a visitor it would be easy to ignore the reality that Arcoverde was located in one of the most socially unequal areas in the world.

I spent most of the afternoon with a few members of the Calixto family outside the bar and cultural space near their cluster of three houses. Assis Calixto, one of the surviving patriarchs of Coco Raízes, was a conscientious host, showing me photo collages hung in their small museum. Sets of matching outfits established the timeline of the group. The first photos, from the mid-1990s, featured an off-white pattern with large, ornate orange and brown blossoms on camp shirts and long, old-fashioned dresses. Later they settled on a lime green and yellow floral print.

Talking to the Calixtos, I began to glimpse the complex network of individuals and institutions, from local to international, that supported this family so revered as bearers of tradition. I asked about a newspaper clipping on the wall about a jazz drummer from Chicago named Andrew Potter, and Assis turned on a boom box to play Potter's instrumental version of Assis's song "Balanço da canoa" (The sway of the canoe). It began with a drum solo that riffed on variations of the two rhythmic cells upon which Coco Raízes's songs are based: the 3+3+2 timeline of *samba de coco* and a fast-paced duple meter of *foguetes de roda*. Soon the other musicians joined in: an electrified upright bass carried the melody, while the chords were filled in on an electric piano. As we listened, Assis sang his lead part, and his nieces, Iuma and Iram, sang their response, which mimicked the sound of waves lapping against a canoe. They clapped along and coaxed his three-year-old nephew Luizinho to demonstrate his prowess at dancing *coco*. Assis pulled a coin from his pocket to sweeten the deal, and the boy hammed it up, stomping remarkably well for one his age.

Meanwhile Iram sat down, irritated by an unproductive meeting about T-shirt designs, muttering something about contracts and verbal commitments that had fallen through. She had the abrupt manner of a businessperson in high demand. Iram was used to interviews, but I was not asking the questions that she usually fielded. This made her impatient. I struggled to come up with a question for her regarding the group's state sponsorship. I had thought that it would take at least a few weeks to become acquainted before launching into my research questions. My position as a long-term visitor would end up being a bit baffling for the musicians to locate. They were unsure whether to treat me as a tourist, a journalist, or just another local attendee of their parties.

Iram's attitude toward her neighborhood during this encounter stood in stark contrast to the reverent manner in which the neighborhood was treated by fans and in the lyrics of Coco Raízes's songs. As I tried to ask another question, a woman on the street walked by with anger in her eyes. She glared at Iram and spat out an insult I did not understand. Initially unruffled by the incident, Iram dismissed it with a wave of her hand, adding, "She's just jealous of us, and our success." Her annoyance grew, however, leading her to repeat that she could no longer stand living on their street and dreamed of buying a house elsewhere so that she could have some peace of mind. She was sick of it all and insisted that these problems with her neighbors were not minor. After debating at length the question of whether the woman was actually insane or merely an awful person, Iram casually mentioned that she was a distant relative. This bitterness was my first taste of the volatility of the success of the *samba de coco* dynasties as the traditional genre had become increasingly lucrative.

My experience on the first day also hinted at how enmeshed the careers of *samba de coco* musicians were with public and private sponsorship. The Calixtos invited me down the hill to their performance at the Social Service of Commerce (SESC), a nonprofit institution managed privately but funded by mandatory public revenue from the commercial sectors of manufacturing, service, and tourism.[2] Its programming is open to all, but its highest priority is to promote the social well-being of the employees within these sectors and their families. The SESC in Arcoverde is a large, well-maintained complex with a cafeteria, a library, exercise machines, an indoor theater, a pool, and an outdoor area for concerts. Paintings on the walls featured various folk forms, including *samba de coco*. I sat outside at a table near the pool for the show. There was no cost for admission, but formally dressed waiters in bow ties circulated through the audience offering platters of hors d'oeuvres.

On stage the musicians and dancers wore matching lime green floral shirts, with the women wearing matching dresses and the men and boys in solid green pants. Ciço Gomes was singing lead, and a pair of young dancers, Fagner Gomes and Daiane Calixto, competed for the attention of the audience. Wearing wooden sandals, they performed a quick, snare drum–like dance step. Unlike, for example, Rio-based contemporary samba, in which dancers move their bodies with *ginga*, or a fluid, graceful swing, *samba de coco* dancers stomp their sandals with force to compete with many loud percussion instruments and amplified voices. Ciço commanded the stage, projecting his resonant voice through the fuzzy, overdriven sound of the PA speakers.

Behind Ciço and the dancers stood three Calixto women singing backup: Iram, her younger sister Iuma, and her mother, Dona Lourdes. The older Calixto men—Assis and his brother Damião—joined the vocal responses, filling out the harmonies while adding precise rhythmic noise with triangle and tambourine.[3] The quick stutter of the *surdo* bass drum, played by Ciço's son François, anchored the shimmering treble. The percussion stayed fixed and tight, other than micro variations in rhythm and timbre caused by the drum, shaker, triangle, tambourine jingles, and wooden sandal stomps suspended in tension with each other. One song's lyrics aptly compared the layers of rhythm to a quickly moving freight train. Indeed, it sounded like a train was speeding over a rickety old wooden bridge. After the show ended Ciço introduced himself and proceeded to pepper me with witty, rapid-fire questions. He turned out to be an affable man in his late forties who performed exuberantly on- and offstage. Ciço laughed easily, his contagious grin accentuated by his mustache.

Everything described in this passage happened during my first day in Arcoverde. I did not compress events that happened over several days; the events were already compressed for me. In other words, I was being warmly received as a tourist. And tourist destinations must regularly and frequently schedule events so that even the shortest-term guest won't arrive, wait for something to happen, and then give up and go elsewhere. My whirlwind first day of research revealed the Calixtos to be professional hosts—so professional that the visitor may not even sense that the hospitality enjoyed was, while not insincere, certainly routine.

Origin Stories

Over the weeks the intertwined origin stories of Coco Raízes and Cordel emerged through conversations with musicians and others who had informally assumed the role of producing the groups. Micheliny introduced me to Rose Mary Gomes de Souza, an insider to the rock and roots music scenes in the city. She in turn introduced me to musicians and invited me to the venues where they performed.

The Bar do Zaca was frequently the place to meet up and listen to live music. Arcoverde was large enough to have several subgroups of artists, but there were not many places to gather, so they coexisted at the Bar do Zaca. There were the "roots" musicians (*música de raíz*), including Alberone Padilha, a member of the original lineup of Cordel who now played in a band that combined fiddle-driven *forró de rabeca* and fife-based *banda de pífano* tunes. His friend Helton Moura, a close friend of Micheliny and Lirinha, straddled the roots and rock music scenes, playing guitar and singing both *mangue beat* and 1970s-style northeastern folk rock such as Alceu Valença and Zé Ramalho. Helton was also part of the radical theater crowd, which had squatted in and claimed the defunct train station in town. The group had adopted the technique of aggressive squatting honed by the MST to turn one of the oldest buildings in town into a spare cultural center run by determined activists offering free art, music, and theater classes for the poor. There were hard rockers and heavy metal enthusiasts playing in bands such as Cobaias (Guinea Pigs) and Biocídio (Biocide). In addition to these loosely formed cliques, older bohemian artists and aficionados in their thirties and forties frequented the outdoor bar. Often there was a table-to-table breakdown of these groups: rockers in the back, theater people (and the lone modern dancer) near the small stage, roots musicians drinking cane liquor on the porch behind the stage, and older bohemians at the tables between the rockers and the actors. Almost everyone present had known each other for many years, if not their whole lives. This intimacy both blurred and accentuated the distinctions between cliques. Lines were blurred in the moments when rockers would playfully heckle Helton's sentimental song choices. Lines were accentuated when old simmering feuds repelled former friends to opposite sides of the yard.

Despite their different passions, the patrons of the Bar do Zaca were united by a common musical enemy: stylized, ultrapopular *forró*, known as *forró estilizado*, which features television-inspired aesthetics, glitzy Las Vegas–style dancers, flashy staging, fog machines, and singers with peppy but often pitchy pop vocal delivery. It was the music usually heard on the principal stage during the São João Festival, on commercial radio stations, and blaring from speaker trucks throughout the city. All of these styles—*forró estilizado*; the more rustic, less flashy *forró pé-de-serra*; *samba de coco*; and various styles of rock and roots music—are still performed each year during the São João Festival in Arcoverde.

Forró estilizado was an unwelcome intruder in the home of artist Suedson

Neiva and his wife Amélia, who worked for the state-sponsored cultural foundation Fundarpe. Suedson and Amélia closed the shutters and told me about the formation of Coco Raízes. Amélia, a student of the Pernambucan cultural preservationist and playwright Ariano Suassuna, was assigned a post in Arcoverde as an outreach coordinator when statewide policy shifted to a platform of decentralization.[4] She also worked for the municipal bureau of culture in Arcoverde. Amélia and Suedson began asking around for any previously active forms of local culture that were ripe to be rescued and supported. They had gotten to know Lula Calixto when he sang *samba de coco* on the street in their neighborhood. Suedson described Lula as "humble, and full of greatness," clarifying that "his simplicity was his greatness." He described how Lula mediated the tense conflicts between group members that were present from the beginning of the revival.

The elderly drummer Biu Neguinho was digging graves for a living when Lula and Amélia went to the cemetery to convince him to dust off his *surdo* bass drum and play again. Biu protested at first, but finally agreed after some convincing. None of the sexagenarians in the newly formed group had danced *coco* in more than fifteen years. Fundarpe provided the group with matching outfits and instruments—and, according to Suedson and Dona Amélia, organized the group at first, before stepping aside and allowing the musicians to choose a new manager and self-govern, a fact that the majority of other accounts of the history of the group omitted or downplayed.

At Home, in the Street, and on the Stage

Ciço Gomes still possessed a few of the videotapes that had survived a small fire in the Calixto home; the fire burned T-shirts, newspaper clips, and several audio- and videotapes. We watched the remaining videos, and Ciço talked about how the group had changed and adapted: "It's very difficult to make the transition between the house, the street and the stage. We are very aware of the difference between these contexts. One has to really make an effort to animate a crowd from the stage. In the beginning, we didn't even have a PA system, just one microphone with a small amplifier. After this, we played on a small stage during São João. We played there, and everyone said 'man, this is great!' and put us on the larger stages."

One of the most striking shifts in the group's performance on stage was the decision to drastically reduce the number of dancers, from around twenty-five to two or three at a time. Fagner, the best young male dancer from the Gomes family, and Daiane, the best young female dancer from the Calixto family, ended up specializing in that role. From that point forward the group's performances were no longer a direct transfer of practices developed in informal, participative contexts. Instead, the circle of dancers broke apart and the musicians faced the audience. Fagner and Daiane served as the group's representatives. They would demonstrate the steps on stage, then jump down into the crowd to coax audience members to dance: "Fagner and Daiane [were the ones who] began this business of getting down from the stage to dance with everyone, snaking through the crowd and getting the circle dance started. It was they who did this." Each larger stage where they performed gave them motivation to rehearse their vocal harmonies and tighten the layers of percussion: "After playing on the largest stages during São João in Arcoverde, they called us to play in Recife, so we went there. We had to realize that we weren't that little group that plays in someone's house anymore. We had to clean up the small mistakes and concentrate harder on really playing well for the stage."

Government cultural preservation efforts and commerce have worked hand in hand in the story of *samba de coco* in Arcoverde. By 2004 recordings of the music of Coco Raízes would serve as the soundtrack to the chamber of commerce convention and a fashion show in the publicly funded colonial district of downtown Recife. Government festivals provided the band with a career ladder to climb as it honed its craft, from local Arcoverde festival stages to Recife's Carnaval.

SAMBA DE COCO *PERFORMED AT HOME*

One of the earliest videotapes from Ciço Gomes's collection contained footage of his daughter's birthday party in 1996, providing an example of an informal performance of *samba de coco* for family and friends, before the group began performing on stage. On the tape the white noise of the shakers, the metallic clang of the triangle, and the staccato booms of the surdo drum enveloped the dancers as they moved in a circle around a small living room cleared of furniture. The percussionists lined the wall behind the circle, and everyone sang the refrains in response to whoever was singing lead at the time. Everyone present was dressed in everyday attire: T-shirts, shorts, trousers, dresses. The mood in the room was of orderly, family-friendly, alcohol-free celebration. The lead singer was alternately Lula Calixto, who was singing in a pinched tone, straining to project over the percussion and the din of voices at the party as he danced in the circle, or Ciço, who stood either in the middle of the circle or outside it. Ciço was constantly making eye contact, singing lines directly to partygoers, lifting people's spirits, and encouraging participation. The force of everyone singing together was more important than the precision of the harmonies, which were roughly parallel thirds. The musicians traded improvised verses, many of which referred to the fact that they were being filmed.

Most of the dancers' steps included a slight shuffle/slide that emulated the swish of the shaker, a touch that was easier to sustain in everyday leather- and rubber-soled shoes than it would be later in wooden sandals, which require an emphatic, precise stomp. There was much more variation in how the dancers accented the basic steps than at later performances on stage. When a song began its rapid-fire *embolada* section, the dancers stopped singing and focused on the quicker-stepped *trupé* dance. While later crowds, such as those in Recife, would take their cues from the dancers on stage, with everyone striving to execute the RlrLrlrl pattern, in this roda some dancers preferred rLrlrLrl, or even Rl.lRı.ı, flowing with or against the grain of the shaker and triangle parts.[5]

The room was small for the thirty or so people who were dancing in it, and the proximity of bodies circulating counterclockwise resembled circles found in *candomblé terreiros* (houses of Afro-Brazilian religion), the initiates packed one after the next, all moving in the same direction around the axis point in the center of the room. In this videotape members of all three families, Lopes, Calixto, and Gomes, were seen celebrating with friends and neighbors—a scene one would not have seen a few years earlier, when the families danced separately, and did not see a few years later, when a family feud had broken out between the Lopeses and Calixtos.

The 1996 video was one of the earliest remaining recordings of the *samba de coco* revival in Arcoverde. The footage had been taken soon after Fundarpe had worked with Lula Calixto to gather the three families of musicians and convince them to resume playing, singing, and dancing *samba de coco*. Prior to this moment certain members of the families had played together before—Lopes and Gomes, for example—but others had not. The revival of *samba de coco* in Arcoverde in the mid-1990s involved the negotiation of musical style. Lula Calixto's notion of the genre included a love for mid-tempo *cocos*, while Ciço Gomes and Biu Neguinho, who had a long history of playing with the Lopes family, would storm through songs at blazing speeds. Biu's previous experience leading a Rio-style samba school influenced his distinctive sticking patterns.

Through their sponsorship, Fundarpe and the SESC cast *samba de coco* as heritage, fitting them within a register of restorative nostalgia. This led to the downplaying of stylistic gaps between *samba de coco* families in order to unite and consecrate the genre as representative of the city. Far from being an easy narrative of progress from the home and the street to the stage, this video merely documents the beginning of the latest chapter in the history of *samba de coco*. After patriarch Ivo Lopes's death in 1987, the musicians stopped playing for the most part, but if one dug deeper into the past, Ivo, Ciço, and Biu were no strangers to public performance. In the 1970s they had mounted shows during the São João Festival with municipal support as well as the sponsorship of beer companies. Ivo had written *cocos* that during that time were popular radio hits, interpreted by *forró* stars such as Genival Lacerda. But the private dimension of the genre, played informally at birthday parties and other family gatherings, continued to be a key site for the music, and in 1996 this recording of the performers without their stage dress provided footage that could be seen as evidence that the genre lived off the stage as well as on it.

FOLKLORE AS A HIGH SCHOOL SCIENCE FAIR PROJECT

The video footage of Dora's birthday party was recorded as part of Micheliny Verunschk's research into *samba de coco* in Arcoverde. During this time Lirinha and the guitarist Clayton Barros accompanied Micheliny as she spoke to musicians who were once a part of the family-centered and semiprivate *coco* salons that had been happening in Arcoverde at least as far back as the 1930s. Lula Calixto taught them about the music and its history and joined them in their efforts to gather more information about how it had been practiced.

The science fair, held at the high school where Lirinha studied, offered students a folklore option, reflecting nineteenth- and early twentieth-century classifications of the study of folklore as a science. At the science fair Lirinha and Clayton performed *samba de coco* and *reisado* repertoire, as well as poetry recitation with guitar accompaniment, on a stage in the cafeteria. The performance was received well enough to garner the attention of the director of the SESC Arcoverde. The SESCs of the state of Pernambuco had been on the lookout for promising, regionally relevant cultural programming that could be sent on tour, and Lirinha and Clayton were invited to produce and rehearse a theatrical folklore revue.

CORDEL'S FIRST PERFORMANCE

A videotape of Cordel's first performance at the SESC begins with the cast walking on stage, illuminated only by open flame kerosene lanterns. Lirinha declares, "Bless Master Chudu," paying tribute to a popular troubadour and poet from a nearby municipality. Before the rest of the show comes on, he recites "O Cordel Estradeiro," asking this dead poet for permission to "become authentic," to "become a messenger of the force of your thunder." Upon Lirinha's uttering the word *verdadeiro* (true or authentic), Clayton Barros played a pleasant, innocuous accompaniment in a major key that underscored this tribute to local elders. But calling for permission from the previous generation of popular poets indicated that, as fledgling performers, their own authenticity in performing this repertoire was in question. This posture of apprenticeship would change drastically as Cordel transformed.

Lirinha defined the performance as a *cordel estradeiro*. The word *cordel* refers to small chapbooks of rhymed poetry or a recited story in general. *Estradeiro* has two meanings. It refers to someone who is almost never at home because he or she is constantly traveling, or to a mule or horse who has a solid, trustworthy gait. By naming their performance a *cordel estradeiro*, Lirinha framed it as tradition made to travel: road-ready folklore. It was a manifesto for the band Cordel, declaring in words and delivery that its artistic gait was trustworthy and solid. After Lirinha asked for permission to represent the tradition of popular poetry and promised to become a messenger for the words of these poets of the *sertão*, he proclaimed, "I, too, am a bandit / And my roadworthy Cordel / Is a powerful rattlesnake." The consonant, reassuring circle-of-fifths chord progression played underneath the claim "I, too am a bandit" frames the moment as the passing of the torch of tradition. At this point the words and music work together to suggest that Cordel's uncertainty is merely the nervousness of novices making their debut. During this early phase, growing up in the area was sufficient to qualify them as culture bearers. This question would become more complicated as they moved away from Arcoverde.

Despite their jitters about performing tradition, at this point Cordel viewed the relationship between interpreter and source material marked as traditional as relatively transparent and free of antagonism. Late in the set one song in particular clearly located Cordel's work within a discourse of loss and recovery:

> Cordel participates in the past
> On a string, the seed is hanging
> Left suddenly
> It has the soul of my *reisado*
> The magic of the enchanted fire
> And the cultural roots of your people
>
> . . . The finest coveted riches
> In the forests of ashes that were green
> In the finest coveted riches
> In the forest of ashes that is Arcoverde
>
> *O cordel participa do passado*
> *Num cordão pendurado a semente*

> *Deixado de repente*
> *Tem a alma do meu reisado*
> *A magia do fogo encantado*
> *E a raiz cultural da sua gente*
>
> *. . . Na mais fina riqueza cobiçada*
> *Nas florestas de cinzas que eram verdes*
> *Na mais fina riqueza cobiçada*
> *Na floresta de cinzas que é Arcoverde*

The audience was told that they had just heard and seen bits and pieces of their cultural heritage—their roots. Cultural forms, such as *samba de coco* and *reisado*, were treated as natural resources. Through an arboreal metaphor of cultural roots—a common comparison within folklore that Cordel would later eschew—the imperative of cultural preservation was reinforced. In the song cultural roots are described as coveted riches almost lost in the scorched earth of modernity, "the forests of ashes that were green." In the last line Arcoverde specifically is pinpointed. The burning of the forest becomes equated with the perceived loss of cultural memory in the city. But these local riches still remain, the song states, and by performing them, together the performers and the audience have helped preserve them.

During the performance these various "cultural riches" were represented —principally poetry and music from what Cordel selected as the local European, African, and indigenous contributions to their cultural identities. At this point Cordel's performance was compatible in many ways with Ariano Suassuna's regionalist Movimento Armorial, which sought to connect with the "magical spirit" of *literatura de cordel* and *sertão* musical styles.

During the show the mood varied from one piece to the next; a satirical poem about a hick bumbling in the city followed a solemn, mystical poem about an indigenous prophecy. Roughly a quarter of the performance consisted of comedic storytelling. This contrasted with later performances of the group, within which it adopted a prophetic, apocalyptic tone for the entire show. Costume changes also signaled the panoramic presentation of the region's forgotten treasures that group members had learned from local culture bearers. During the last third of the performance the group further reinforced the posture of homage by donning colorful folk Catholic *reisado* outfits and performing a medley of more than ten songs from the repertoires of local *reisado* and *samba de coco* groups. During a slower, hymnlike *reisado* song, the members of Cordel dramatized the Catholic context of this performance by kneeling and putting their hands together in a gesture of prayer. At the end of the performance the mostly middle-aged and elderly patrons of the institution seated in the SESC theater clapped politely, in stark contrast to the screaming, cheering, singing, and moshing of the young fans that Cordel would later mesmerize at outdoor festivals.

From the Theater to the Festival

Soon after Cordel's first performance, the group caught the attention of two prominent culture brokers in Pernambuco's state capital, Recife: Antonio Gutierrez, known as Gutie, and Juvenal de Holanda Vasconcelos, known as Naná Vasconcelos. Gutie produces Rec-Beat, a large festival within Recife's Carnaval celebration, featuring a combination of Brazilian and foreign acts performing international pop styles, local acts performing regional traditional styles, and groups inspired by *mangue beat*, which combined both categories. Naná Vasconcelos is a percussionist who is internationally known for his participation in avant-garde, proto–"world music" recordings on the ECM record label during the late 1970s and early 1980s, as well as his collaboration on Paul Simon's *Rhythm of the Saints* record. He has repeatedly played the role of "the traditional" or even "the primitive" in pieces that juxtapose folklore and experimentalist contemporary art music, such as one scored for percussion, nonverbal vocalizations, and string quartet. His celebrations of the elemental presaged the themes of New Age music in the 1980s and 1990s; his work represents an optimistic strain of modernist primitivism circulating in the avant-pop/jazz world.

Cordel was taken under Gutie's wing, and Naná produced the group's first record. When it moved to Recife, only the singer Lirinha and the guitarist Clayton Barros, the two principal songwriters, remained from the original lineup; two percussionists, Nego Enrique and Rafa Almeida, who grew up playing in *candomblé terreiros* in the poverty-stricken Morro da Conceição neighborhood of Recife, joined the band, as well as Emerson Calado, a drummer from Arcoverde's hard rock scene. No longer marketed as a folkloric theater troupe, the group was now playing at festival stages along with other groups lumped under the umbrella category *mangue beat*. As early as 2001, in press interviews Lirinha expressed growing discomfort with the idea of cultural rescue, as well as with Cordel's music being branded as regional. Lirinha began to refer to their earlier posture as gatherers of folklore as an "epoch of homage" that had since passed: "We don't want to work with the revival, rescue [*resgate*] or rereading of traditional sounds. I don't know even if we will end up finding what we're looking for, which is to make music that is ever more closely derived from individual emotions. This principle breaks the idea of a sound limited to a certain region or, then, with the language of a certain region. An accent, we know, is what is inevitable."

Naná Vasconcelos urged Emerson Calado to explore nontraditional techniques on instruments with conventional roles in marginal-turned-traditional music. Naná was famous for exploring unorthodox ways to play the one-stringed musical bow the *berimbau*, and Emerson followed his lead by transferring his loud, heavy sensibility developed in hard rock and metal bands to *surdo*, *alfaia*, and *zabumba* drums. Although it is difficult to parse how much of their new sound was due to the new lineup, how much of it was Gutie's production guidance, and how much of it was the influence of Naná's aesthetics, all these factors are present in Cordel's move away from the ascetic aesthetics of folklore. Cordel now had an elaborate lighting system at its disposal and a sound engineer to trigger samples and add sound effects. All the instruments were miked, and the mix emphasized thunderous bass, visceral percussion, and Lirinha's apocalyptic incantations.

While the first performance in Arcoverde began with a call for dead poets to authenticate the work of the group, its first CD and performances on the subsequent tour began with the more nebulous, disorienting track "A chegada do Zé do Né na lagoa de dentro" (The arrival of Zé do Né to the inner lagoon). The track started with sound in the left channel and floated to the right as the reverse attack of an acoustic guitar's decay played backward built to an abrupt crescendo. Immediately after this first guitar stab, a vocal melismatic melody appeared as the guitar continued to orbit from ear to ear. Clayton's guitar playing recorded backward sustained a low drone while he picked quicker notes on the upper strings, which when reversed sounded like prickly stabs. The prolonged attack of the droning low notes gave the song an expansive sense of space, invoking the Doppler effect and sounding like a recording made in slow motion. The detail of the lilting *aboio* (an a capella cowherder's song) that the singer Zé do Né recorded with the crackly aesthetic of early ethnographic field recording, was contrasted with the swirling guitar recorded backward.[6] Once the looped vocal sample repeated itself verbatim, however, its electronic manipulation was foregrounded, and it too was denaturalized and unmoored in this swirling orbit.

By the time Cordel's tours were being produced by Gutie and their disc was recorded by Naná, the band had gone from downplaying the intertextual gaps between its performances and those of related performers to emphasizing gaps in order to present the group as iconoclastic innovators. The band's shift away from a posture of homage was vividly indexed by the changes in the performance of "O Cordel Estradeiro," with which they began their first SESC show. The song, which declares their performance to be "road-ready folklore," indexes the band's emerging questions about the use of marginal-turned-traditional source materials. The song, in which

Lirinha calls to his departed elders in the world of poetry and popular culture for authentication, now explores the negative potential of homage, understood as an appropriation rather than a tribute. Although Lirinha recites more or less identical words, the difference becomes clear the moment he utters the word *verdadeiro* (authentic). During the band's earlier performances the guitar came in to reassure the audience with a pleasant, stable chord progression. On the record, however, an ominous, dissonant line appears at this point, using the lowest register of an accordion run through distortion and other effects.[7] What appeared earlier to be the inspirational passing of the torch of tradition now sounds like a Frankenstein-like jolting of life into the dead. With the recitation of the image of Lirinha's land as a rugged place where "the rattlesnake naps in the mouth of the bandit," the *aboio* sample of "Zé do Né" reappears, this time played backward.

With this contrasting musical accompaniment, the tone of the poem shifts from Lirinha reverently asking for his elder's blessing to asserting his power with bluster. Cordel's new power is declared with a show of technical prowess by playing the sampled traditional voice backward—like a magic show, in which a magician, with a puff of smoke, suspends someone upside down in midair. Just as the magician performing such a trick would control the inverted body, Cordel asserts control over the traditional material.

After this act of self-authentication Lirinha's own words are once again blurred with moments of ventriloquism. Now when he recites another poet's verse, the mood shifts abruptly as a sunny circle of fifths chord progression emerges. In the CD liner notes these poets are cited without quotation marks, and during performance it isn't clear where Lirinha's words end and the other poets' verses begin. When the last verse ended during Cordel's debut performance, the song ended. But on the CD, the moment that the words are complete the dark accordion part returns, along with the inverted *aboio* vocal sample. Musically and lyrically, the band acknowledges in this track that its approach could be heard as either homage to be celebrated or appropriation to be scorned.

This marked change in its posture of homage happened during the period when many of the traditional performers cited in Cordel's lyrics and music were approaching the band with intellectual property rights claims. The half hour of *samba de coco* and *reisado* songs from their Arcoverde phase had been whittled down to one four-minute medley, chosen because it consisted of songs in Arcoverde's *samba de coco* and *reisado* repertoires that were played by other groups throughout the region, making them impervious to lawsuits claiming ownership of the song's intellectual property rights. The excessive footnotes in the CD booklet, citing details as minute as the fact that the rhythm of a made-up word was inspired by a *samba de coco* dancer's steps, serve two purposes: (1) to prevent lawsuits in Arcoverde's volatile environment by acknowledging the band's sources and (2) to prove the band's uniqueness in the musical marketplace by linking it to the interior region in a way no coastal Recife band can claim.

In addition to the shrinking of the folkloric medleys, the structure of the performances shifted during Cordel's second phase, when the band members were living in Recife. While Cordel was starting out in Arcoverde the mood on stage would vary from one skitlike segment to the next. Following a poem about an indigenous prophecy, Lirinha would tell a funny story about a bumbling rural man trying to navigate the urban environment. Humorous poems followed solemn moments. After moving away from Arcoverde, however, the mood of a few moments in the first performance, in which Lirinha portrayed the charismatic power of the prophets and the bandits, became standard throughout the entire show. Humor was almost completely absent, and the majority of the words were spoken as an incantation, or "a heavy church mass" as the band described it in its lyrics. An aura of ecstatic religion was invoked through the use of *candomblé* drumming patterns in 12/8 time, folk Catholic pilgrim's songs, and the impassioned vocal cadence of a millenarian fire and brimstone preacher.

The last scene of the band's music video for "Chover (ou invocação para um dia liquido)" (Rain [Invocation for a liquid day]), which enjoyed MTV Brasil airplay, was filmed under the cross of the Alto do Cruzeiro. The clip featured Cordel and the Calixto family dancing *coco* and playing music together. This image of harmony and celebration belied the instability of their relationship at that time, as each group was finding a way through distinct but tethered predicaments surrounding their emerging commodification. The musicians in Coco Raízes were working to realize their dreams of appearing on television and performing all over Brazil. As they worked toward these goals, they were aware that they were performing music with premodern roots within a place-based project. In the words of their stage manager, Carlinhos, Coco Raízes had to remain careful not to "get off track" by revealing their ambitions and risk being seen as just another pop band. The members of Coco Raízes maintained their floral print, old-fashioned outfits for performing and reluctantly heeded their manager's warning not to abandon Arcoverde as their home base. Meanwhile, Cordel faced a transition from folklore revue to mutationist pop band and, in percussionist Emerson Calado's words, eased away from reproducing the work of others, toward producing original work of its own. Authorship copyright conflicts only accelerated the movement of both groups away from drawing inspiration from songs considered part of the public domain.

CHAPTER TWO

Museums

When Lula Calixto died on November 15, 1999, his death triggered a social earthquake, shifting the tectonic plates of the *samba de coco* families in Arcoverde. Almost immediately friction emerged between the Calixto and Gomes families on one side and the Lopes sisters on the other.

Lula Calixto's Death and a Feud Fought through Museums

The strain on the relationship among the three families was evident as early as Lula's funeral. Assis lent me a videotape of the memorial service, which took place at the gymnasium of the SESC. In the middle of the gym floor, the casket was open, and Lula's body was completely covered by a layer of daisies. Only his face was visible, and his trademark leather hat was placed on the flowers. Padim Batista's pífano band stood around the coffin and played mournful waltzes on fife and percussion. Mayor Rosa Barros, Lirinha and Clayton from Cordel, union leaders, people holding flags from the MST, teachers, and students came to pay their respects. Up above on a balcony stood students holding a banner, which read: "The Carlos Rios school mourns their good friend 'Lula Calixto,' even knowing that the artist doesn't die." Down below union members held a banner that read: "Lula Calixto. Symbol of struggle and resistance for his roots. Sintepe [the union's name]." Onlookers stepped back as clowns on stilts paid tribute to Lula by precariously circling the open coffin. A priest led prayers and songs, the mayor spoke, and around Lula's body the *samba de coco* group, dressed to perform, did a somber rendition of the normally ebullient dance.

All thirty or so members of the group at the time were dressed to perform in matching floral print shirts and dresses. All members except Severina Lopes, that is, who came to the funeral not in a floral dress, but in a plaid vest and pants. Damião Calixto interpreted this choice as an act of defiance, which triggered the ensuing power struggle. To members of the Calixto family, Severina setting herself apart from the rest of the group and wearing a vest—one of Lula's trademark clothing choices—was her signal to the rest of the group that she was claiming control of the group, which at the time bore her brother Ivo Lopes's name.[1]

Severina remembered the sequence of events differently. To her, the first indication that the group would splinter surfaced a few days later, at a live interview on a local radio station regarding Lula's legacy and the future of the group. In her version of the story, Damião Calixto asserted his power in response to the DJ's question about what would happen to *samba de coco* in Arcoverde after Lula's death. Damião said: "The *coco* now is mine. It belongs to my daughter [Iram], to my wife [Dona Lourdes] and to my brother [Assis]." Severina kept a cassette copy of the broadcast as evidence. It was devastating to her, she explained, not only because of this declaration, but because he went on to say, on the radio, that he was taking over the *coco* because he claimed the sisters weren't strong singers and dancers.

Lula's death was followed by a surge of media coverage in Arcoverde and Recife, depicting him as a beloved hero of popular culture. Lula's status vaulted from town eccentric and street vendor to artist and local figure of cultural resistance. His family, who had previously been ambivalent about his passion for *samba de coco*, perceived that both the music and the Calixto name were valuable currencies.

Soon after Lula's death a van paid for by the municipal government came to pick up the musicians and take them to a recording studio. According to Severina's version of events, there was space in the van for ten people, but thirteen people were present. Damião rebuffed the Lopes sisters by ushering some of his younger children into the van and then telling the sisters that there were no seats left. Being shut out of the recording process was the breaking point that formalized the rift between the Lopes and Calixto families. The Gomes family, who had played *samba de coco* with the Lopes family since the early 1960s, were caught in the middle and ended up siding with the Calixtos.

Damião's harsh assessment of the Lopes sisters' musical abilities offers an entry into a cluster of issues regarding musical professionalism, cultural patrimony, and authorship rights that converged around Lula's death. The conflict between the families centered on claims to the title of Arcoverde's *samba de coco* tradition. The clash over these competing claims to tradition and authenticity was also a conflict over the criteria used to judge which family deserved its crown. The Calixto and Gomes families, committed to professionalizing, insisted on frequent rehearsals to hone their vocal harmonies, choreography, and percussion skills. The Lopes sisters balked at so much rehearsal, arguing that they knew the repertoire because they had been playing it for years in their late brother Ivo Lopes's group. For the Lopes sisters, their claim to the title was based on the fact that their brother had been playing *samba de coco* in Arcoverde since the early 1950s. They considered the honor to be a patrimony of their family, and believed that no amount of rehearsal could change that immutable truth.

The Calixto family could stake their claim on the fact that they had danced *samba de coco* privately at family gatherings and had attended events throughout their lives. They did not, however, have a *samba de coco* group with a long history of public performances as Ivo Lopes had. Despite this lack, a curious thing happened: the increased attention paid to Lula Calixto by Fundarpe, the municipal government, and subsequently Cordel, forged the association between the Calixto family name and the *samba de coco* tradition. His death only served to consecrate this link further in the eyes of the public. Although the other Calixtos had begun to dance and play *samba de coco* in an organized fashion only after Lula Calixto and Fundarpe's Dona Amélia brought the group together in the mid-1990s, they became emblematic of the unbroken transmission of tradition in Arcoverde from generation to generation.

In addition to conflicts over professionalism and patrimony, race was a largely unspoken factor underlying the public's anointing of the Calixtos as the public representatives of Arcoverde's living folk traditions. Although all three families are mixed race, like the majority of families in Northeast Brazil, the Calixtos are darker skinned and perceived as phenotypically Afro-Brazilian, while the Lopes family is lighter skinned and considered *mestiço*. In the 1990s, unlike in the 1950s through early 1970s, which were the heyday of Ivo Lopes's group, *samba de coco* in Arcoverde struck a chord with Recifenses and other outsiders in part because of its distinctive Afro-Brazilian feel in the midst of the *mestiço* cowboy culture dominant in the *sertão*. At performances I often heard comments that the Calixto family must have originally come to the *sertão* as part of a quilombo community of escaped slaves, highlighting the fact that the Calixtos' skin tone was dark enough by *sertão* standards to be deemed worthy of remark.[2] A local Afrocentric newspaper, *Abibiman*, frequently highlighted the story of *samba de coco* in its pages, featuring articles on a local example of Afro-Brazilian culture that deserved to be celebrated.

After the prospect of making a career out of *coco* began to appear viable, the Calixto family pushed to professionalize the group. The popularity of Cordel was on the rise throughout Pernambuco, raising the *samba de coco* musicians' expectations of their prospects. The *samba de coco* group, then called A Caravana de Ivo Lopes, had recently participated in a Recife-based compilation CD. Lula's dream of recording a CD was about to be realized, since Arcoverde's mayor, Rosa Barros, had agreed to provide financial support and transportation to Recife for the recording. At the last group meeting that Lula attended, Severina Lopes had signed documents authorizing the group to record several of her brother's songs.

The feud deepened when the first pressing of CDs arrived and Severina Lopes was contacted to sign a release form. In the bureaucratic paperwork establishing the group as an official association, which was necessary to receive government support, Severina Lopes was still listed as the group's leader. Now estranged from the current group and in the process of establishing her own rival group, she vehemently refused to sign off on a recording that included four songs she claimed were written by her brother Ivo. In his account of the feud, Ciço Gomes, the lead singer of the Calixto/Gomes group that had changed their name to Coco Raízes, countered that some of the songs actually predated Ivo Lopes's group, and that others had been written collaboratively when he sang in Ivo's group years before. Ciço also questioned what constituted authorship in a genre in which improvisation played such a prominent role. Severina held her ground, and the CDs were withheld from the market until three thousand more were printed without the songs in question, reducing the track count from sixteen to twelve.

From this time forth, questions of authorship and intellectual property became highly contested among Arcoverde's traditional musicians. The split and feud took place during the broader neoliberal developments in Brazil, which included a "drive to classify most forms of expressive and material culture as IP and then stringently 'protect' them" (Dent 2012, 34). Anxious responses to the emerging centrality of piracy could be found throughout Brazil, as well as much of the rest of the world. But for the *samba de coco* families, a push to secure legitimate avenues of circulation for their recordings, rather than having the product of their labor be consumed as royalty-less pirated wares sold on the street, coincided with their efforts to emerge out of the anonymous periphery of the Brazilian backlands.

Severina recruited young musicians to create the Coco Irmãs Lopes and threatened to sue Coco Raízes if they sang any songs that were on the list of those she claimed Ivo Lopes had written. These threats were often made on stage from the microphone at gigs where both groups were scheduled to play. The feud played out in the court of public opinion. Maintaining close ties with both groups became difficult in this combative climate. When Sandroni's project retracing the steps of Mário de Andrade's musical fieldwork recorded Coco Irmãs Lopes, Severina insisted on prefacing each song being recorded with, "This next song, which Ivo Lopes also wrote, is entitled . . ." before the group could begin playing.

The concept of *intriga* outlined in Ana Claudia Marques's ethnography of social conflict in the Pernambucan *sertão* closely conforms to the intrigue at Lula's funeral, at the radio station, and as the van pulled away. Marques defines an *intriga* as the events that spark a *briga de famílias*, a family feud. Once the *intriga* has stoked the feud, it becomes a *questão*: an ongoing pattern of confrontation and retaliation between family members and their allies. In her words, "An *intriga* is a moment that projects the *questão* from the past into the present, in the direction of the future" (Marques 2002, 22; author's translation). Many of the protagonists of the feuds that Marques analyzes are landowning patriarchs—"founders of a lineage and a place" (Marques 2002, 21)—and the patterns of vengeance to restore honor are most famously told in the legend of the bandit Lampião, who hailed from Serra Talhada, a Pernambucan municipality near Arcoverde. How the conflict between the Calixto and Lopes families played out could be seen as an echo of these larger, more notorious conflicts in the region's history. Although volatile, the Calixto/Lopes conflict was fought with bitter words and competing museums, not violence. Instead of land or financial capital, of which both families had relatively little at that point, they fought over the prestigious and potentially lucrative symbolic capital of being known as founders of a musical lineage. They guarded their family's musical patrimony as if it were acres of fertile land. Their *questão* drew a line in the sand, delineating and intensifying alliances. The feud bolstered solidarity within each group as they closed their ranks and wooed sympathetic outsiders by inviting them to hear their side of the story.

Severina's most ambitious effort to sustain the memory of Ivo Lopes and the Lopes family's link to *samba de coco* is a museum that she set up in the front porch of the house where she lived with her immediate family and her two sisters, Leni and Josefa. The following extensive description of a visit to the Ivo Lopes Museum provides a glimpse of the idiosyncrasies of nostalgia deployed both in the service of procuring government support for Severina's *coco* group and for more personal reasons. Her fond childhood memories from the "good old days"—and the sparkle in her eye was undeniable as she fell into a storytelling reverie—were interspersed with memories of the "bad old days" when certain families ruled the region with an authoritarian hand. Personal mementos that triggered nostalgia, such as photos and artifacts no longer useful in today's world, also served as evidence in the Lopes sisters' case proving their family's investment in tradition. Legal and quasi-legal documents such as depositions and notarized documents occupied space in picture frames alongside photos of families dancing and playing music.

"Who Has the Roots?": A Visit to the Ivo Lopes Museum

Antigamente—in the olden days—Severina explained, her family used to sit on the ground without a table and eat without forks. They made couscous in a two-tiered clay pot and ate beans and rice from a clay dish. The clay dish made them taste better. There was no electricity—they used various kinds of lanterns, including one made with a small glass bottle, a strip of rag, kerosene, and a bottle cap with a hole in it. She jumped up from her rocking chair and identified artifacts on shelves and hanging on the walls of her front porch/museum. Severina and her older, quieter sister Leni, sitting in the rocking chair next to her, were both close to seventy years old. When Severina demonstrated practices of yesteryear, like the process of drying, roasting, and pounding coffee beans using a mortar and pestle, her face became animated. She had a large sifter that she first used to illustrate how to sift manioc flour and then handed to her young granddaughter so that she could hesitantly dance a step using the sifter as a prop.

Severina invited me to take a look around. A clay jug, clay cooking pots, a stone grinder, and a large mortar were arranged on the floor next to the wall (see figures 2.1 and 2.2). The mortar, whittled from a single log, stood thigh-high, plastic flowers spilling out from its hollowed-out cup. On the adjacent wall hung pieces of metal tools—a shovel, a saw, a hoe, a trowel, a pickaxe, a sickle, a drill bit, a cement spreader, and an axe—covered in rust, abandoned by their wooden handles, which appeared to have long since rotted away. These objects, whether made of clay, iron, or wood, were weathered and encrusted. The clay jugs and cooking pots were dusty and sooty due to age and use. The log mortar was dried and gray. From floor to ceiling there was a progression from tarnished to shiny—from old to new.

The next level of objects, displayed on the walls above the clay, stone, wood, and metal, were tightly woven rattan sifters. Blue, green, and yellow ribbons were draped from the sifters, signaling that these were not functional, but instead props for the "sifter dance." Moving up the wall from the festooned sifters, several straw and leather hats were arranged. One small straw hat with lace trim had yarn braids attached, identifying it as part of a Saint John's Day hick costume. Three conical straw hats approximated the headwear of a nearby indigenous group. A leather hat was painted with the words "Coco do Ivo Lopes." Above the hats, on a shelf near the ceiling, were trophies from the 1960s and 1970s commemorating the group's participation in town-sponsored cultural events, such as *coco* dancing contests.

I began to see patterns in how things were arranged. The clay jars and cooking pots were almost treated like fossils made of materials closer to the earth than today's stainless steel. Moving my gaze up the wall told me a tale that developed from the earth, to functional tools made from the earth, to the transition from function to art seen in the sifter dance prop, to the costume hats, and ending near the ceiling with the social recognition they

Figure 2.1. Artifacts in the Lopes family museum. *Photo by the author.*

received for *fazendo cultura* (making culture), as many traditional musicians called it.

To the left of the wall of hats and sifter props stood two black metal shelves. Next to the ground, on the lowest shelf, more clay mixing bowls and blackened clay cooking pots were placed. On the next shelf above the bowl was a 1960s suitcase-style portable phonograph, sharing the shelf with an old Luiz Gonzaga record featuring the "King of Baião" wearing his trademark leather hat. Above the cooking pots sat a rusty, hand-crank-driven sewing machine, an iron heated with hot coals, a cast iron teakettle, and a miniature wooden ox cart complete with carved oxen. Moving upward to the third shelf, above the phonograph stood Ivo's old radio with three porcelain hens on top of it.

Draped from the posts of the shelves were name tags from events Severina had attended, including a conference for "entrepreneurs of culture" and a badge proving she was a cast member with a speaking part in the internationally famous, Oscar-nominated, and Golden Globe–winning film *Central Station*. The top shelf displayed a large polka dot pincushion used for handweaving lace. From floor to ceiling, I again gathered a sense of upward movement, from the earth to tools to modern technology, and a movement from the faraway rural past, through Ivo's group's heyday up to Severina's present life as a cultural entrepreneur and featured actor in an internationally acclaimed film. But perhaps this was simply how I began

Figure 2.2. Rising up, from clay pots to trophies. *Photo by the author.*

to connect the dots between the disparate, unmarked objects carefully arranged throughout the room—like the similarities I noticed between the shape of the straw hats on the opposite wall and that of the bell-like PA loudspeaker sitting in the corner.

Above the doorway to the right, leading from the front porch museum to the rest of the house, hung a golden sign commemorating the group's fifty-year anniversary and a large, retouched photo of Ivo Lopes. Next to the sign three ragdolls were displayed beside the leather hat of a well-known local *forró* musician who had recently died. Above the dolls was mounted an antique pistol aiming toward the "fifty years" sign. A *berimbau* decorated in colors representing Afrocentrism occupied the space surrounding the dolls, along with a pink porcelain crane and a toy hot-air balloon suspended on fishing line over the doorway.[3] Following the balloon's imagined path upward led my eye to the painted Styrofoam Brazilian flag on the ceiling, stars spilling off the flag and spreading out overhead.

Way back when, Severina continued, the Lopes family would dance *coco* after the *novenário*. In the beginning of May they would erect a maypole, and every night for thirty-one nights they would pray; after they were done they would light a bonfire to keep the snakes away and dance *coco* from around nightfall until midnight or beyond. On the last day of May they would pull down the maypole; it was said that when it toppled, whoever managed to grab the white flag that had been flying at the top of it would marry that year. Severina grabbed it when she was fourteen, but she did not end up marrying that year. "The old days were beautiful, because we didn't use instruments. Everything was based on yelling and the sound of the tin can shaker." She found the rusty can that she had on display and showed it to me. "It's not the actual one," she clarified, "but it's like the cans they used to use." She continued:

> Those days were beautiful because all you used to hear was the hollering of the women and the men. The whole night. When the sun came up, you had mud up to your knees. It was beautiful. Because of the lantern, when the sun came up, your nostrils were full of black soot. That was beautiful.
>
> Now, I think *coco* today is great too, because it has been rescued, the culture of it, with instruments like the shaker, the triangle, the bass drum. They used to use a scraper, like that one you see right there [pointing to the wall of artifacts]. It is nice too, but the old days were better. People were innocent then. You didn't see what you see today at parties. You organize a nice party, and Mr. so-and-so ends the fun by starting a fight. You know that these days there is lots of violence.

Severina's comparisons between the "good old days" and the present took a turn when she began to lament current legal limitations on the freedom to dole out frontier justice: "Back then, I remember as a young girl, if a guy was drunk and noisy, it wasn't a problem. My grandparents and uncles got together and tied up the hands and feet of the troublemaker and stuck him there at the side of the party, tied up until he sobered up."

When her family moved to Arcoverde, she explained, it was not even called Arcoverde. When they arrived the area was almost completely forested. She inventoried the changes, from the town's three names, to the fact that the first cemetery is now a parking lot, to the presence of a gas station in the center of town. People used to be required to wear blue or red ribbons on the brims of their hats to indicate their political alliances. The Brito family was in power until around 1950. The family's henchmen kept everyone in line, and no one could do anything about it. Severina's sister Leni chimed in that a tree trunk that had thick iron hoops on it for shackling slaves to be punished still stood at a nearby plantation.

Surveying the collection, Severina admitted that many of the antiques were not actually Ivo's possessions, or her family's for that matter, but were meant to represent the kinds of things that people had back then. "When I decided to set up this museum, I ate out of aluminum plates and used a gas stove. What was I supposed to do?" She clarified, "You know, at the time, when you replaced your old stove with a newer one, you just threw it into the forest. You had no idea you would end up wanting it back for any reason."

A family photographic portrait in shades of brownish grey had been taken outside in the *sertão*, with a backdrop of mountains and a swirl of clouds. Ivo Lopes stood in the center of the photo, a huge man, twice as wide as any other family member. Three people stood above and behind the other Lopes family members, on some kind of pedestal that was blocked from view. The man in the middle of the back row held a guitar. In the frame of the picture, their shoulders lined up with the top of the mountains. Their faces faded into the clouds, due to the photo's age or a glitch in the developing process. The ghostly musician hovered above the family members standing obediently with patient, serious expressions on their faces. In the corner of the photograph the year 1981 was written, a full half-century later than my mental estimate of its age.

When I showed an interest in the portrait, Severina took out boxes containing more photos of her family. Many of the color photos were of her grandchildren in costumes, whether dressed as the Virgin Mary in a church pageant; as a pigtailed, freckle-faced hick for Saint John's Day; as a wizard to get drivers' attention as part of school patrol duties; or in the colorful, embroidered *coco* outfit. Severina pointed to pictures of her granddaughter and said, "I like it that she does this kind of thing. I think it's beautiful. I think it's culture." After these more recent photos, she passed me some older family portraits. Two startling pictures had the figure of a person sliced out and another placed behind it so that a second face peered through the silhouette-shaped gap in the first photo. The replacement photos were shot at much closer range, so that one eye fit where the missing person's head would have been, as if someone were peering through an unusually shaped keyhole. I asked Severina why the photos looked like this, and she replied that she had been in a feud with a relative. Eventually, after they made amends, she had felt the need to place her relative once more in the family portraits.

Severina brought out file after file of photocopied documents. There were documents stamped and signed by a notary public that declared she was part of the leadership of the *samba de coco* group that had included the Lopes, Gomes, and Calixto families before the feud. There were also documents filled with signatures, many of them written by small children. These papers were the minutes from her new *coco* group's rehearsals, part of a paper trail she hoped would help them secure the municipal government's support for the group and museum. Leni explained that if government auditors were to ask them for evidence of the sustained month-to-month activity of the group, they would have it. Another set of papers, the oldest, was composed of fragments of legal documents from 1974 registering her brother Ivo's song titles and lyrics. Some of the papers were intact, but most had been ripped up in a rage by a relative in the midst of a family dispute.

Typed depositions from city councilmen, neighbors, and family members regarding Ivo Lopes's *coco* group were framed on the wall. Some stated that they had seen the Lopes family dancing *coco* in the rural area where they lived before coming to Arcoverde, and others confirmed that Ivo had been playing as early as the 1950s, reiterating the cultural value of the group for the town. At one point Severina turned to the sign over the doorway and restated the Lopes family claim over that of the Calixtos: "Who has the roots? Seven years or fifty years?"

Taxidermied Goats and Wire-and-Rag Birds:
The Lula Calixto Cultural Space

The first time I met the Calixto family, I spent the afternoon with them eating cream crackers and raw sugar outside the Lula Calixto Cultural Space. It was a garage-like room arranged as a museum, across the street from the Calixto family homes. Lula Calixto's personal belongings were displayed on the walls and on a table next to an open guest book. There was Lula's flugelhorn, which he played for decades in the town band, and wire-and-rag sculptures of animals he made for use in his carnaval group. He called the group a *bloco zoológico*, in which Lula and kids from the community would parade down the main street as a costumed menagerie. In front of a large tapestry hand painted with the group's name stood an almost life-sized patchwork ox; a rooster in disrepair and a half-finished bird (a vulture?) hung on the wall, as well as a chicken-wire frame that he was in the process of making when he died. Next to the wire-and-rag animals stood a taxidermied goat on a skateboard made, Assis told me, by one of the Calixto boys. The skateboard was painted with the inscription "Bob's Goat," and the goat wore a wig of dreadlocks, revealing that the "Bob" in question was reggae great Bob Marley (see figure 2.3).

Through the use of taxidermy, rather than wire frames and cloth, Bob's Goat took Lula's menagerie in a new direction that was meant as playful, but was seen by some visitors as monstrous. When a camera crew from TV Globo later went to great lengths to avoid filming it, it stood outside the desired profile for televised images of patrimony, rurality, and tradition. As I explore further in the epilogue, it was unclear whether the cameraman was avoiding the goat because of the playful use of taxidermy, or because the references to skateboarding and Bob Marley punctured the imagined premodernity being depicted.

Figure 2.3. The taxidermied Bob Marley goat in between wire animals in the Calixto Cultural Space. *Photo by the author.*

A display assembled for the funeral was now leaning against the wall in the cultural space: a large photo of Lula in his leather hat, his eyes turned skyward as in a religious painting; his flutes; and texts written in memory of him. A banner for his *bumba-meu-boi* group was propped up in the corner. Photo collages of musicians and dancers in busy floral print clothes hung on the wall, including pictures of Cordel's lead singer Lirinha as a teenager, back when he played *samba de coco* with the Calixtos. As I looked at the photos, Assis told me about the events at which a given photo was taken, or, based on the color of the matching outfits, the approximate year. Near the back corner were two striking black-and-white photographs of Lula standing in a doorway in the half-light, the contrast sharpened between darks and lights. Assis Calixto volunteered that the pictures had been taken by a French photographer and sent back to the family after his visit.

Competing Cabinets of Curiosities

The Lopes Museum and the Calixto Cultural Space attracted visitors, giving the families an opportunity to charm them, tell their stories about *samba de coco* in Arcoverde, and win over new advocates and fans. In the

Lopes Museum Severina uses a dense array of objects displayed in her front porch to fashion a narrative asserting her family's place in the history of the town. As opposed to an institutionally curated categorization of artifacts, as one would expect to find in a public museum, the configuration of Severina's selected objects on display betrays a more personal logic. Severina is a self-described "wildcat of culture" (to quote the inscription under the wildcat pelt mounted in the museum), defending her family's claim to the establishment of a musical lineage by using objects from previous eras. Her use of the past, however, is not simply a backward gaze, but builds connections leading from the past to the present and into the future. It indexes an agricultural past and celebrations of a previous era in order to chart the movement toward *samba de coco*'s second life as heritage, a representative cultural "survival" celebrated today. Not only is this trajectory an appreciation of the past, but this process of cobbling together past artifacts and practices offers a way to glimpse better times to come, a future contained in a dream of social recognition, as if floating in a hot-air balloon up into the realm of nationwide visibility. The radio, phonograph, and loudspeakers dislocate the sounds of rural northeasterners from their sources—Luiz Gonzaga being the most famous example—and projects them beyond their places of origin and into the national (and international) spotlight. And like Luiz Gonzaga, this projection is accomplished by playing music while wearing costumes. When Severina pointed to photos of her granddaughter all dressed up and stated, "I think it's culture," she was using a local inflection of the word *cultura* referring to creative expressions that lead to recognition in the public sphere, including the educated classes and mass media. In this dream of *fazendo cultura* within such a rigid, racialized class structure, changing hats and outfits and changing one's status are powerfully, allegorically intertwined.[4]

The more frequently visited Calixto Cultural Space contrasted with the Lopes Museum's barrage of objects; when visitors arrived, the focus within the space remained more firmly on the Calixto family members present during the visit. The photos of Lula framed on the wall and his personal effects and extravagant animal creations facilitated talking about Lula and established his importance to the family and the group. By August 2004 the group's projection beyond Arcoverde, and beyond even Brazil, was gaining momentum, as a French producer had offered them a European tour. Coco Raízes were enjoying ample attention from fans, visitors, and the media, and as a result the Cultural Space did not radiate the same will to convince the visitor that the notarized documents in the Lopes Museum represent.

In many ways the two exhibits resonated with the layouts of the Kunstkammern, or cabinets of curiosities, popular in Europe between 1540 and

1740. I mention the Kunstkammern because, like the Lopes and Calixto spaces—and unlike modern museums—the Kunstkammern combined an adulation of noble families and a delineation of the territory of their reign with a collection of objects divided into several categories (natural history, art history, tools and technology, both obsolete and current). Also, Kunstkammern were arranged so as to imply a progressive sequence of stages. In Samuel Quiccheberg's outline of the Kunstkammer, from 1565, these stages developed "from natural objects through ancient sculptures and modern forms of art, and finally to technical instruments and machines" (Bredekamp 1995, 30). A similar kind of implicit narrative of progression is found in Severina Lopes's front porch, moving from clay pots to decorated sifter props to phonographs and proof of participation in filmmaking. In addition, Kunstkammern tended to be arranged to downplay the strict delineation of categories of objects displayed, with the goal of acknowledging and mimicking the playfulness of God's creative process. The boundaries blurred by the alignment of a taxidermied goat in a dreadlocked wig on a skateboard next to a wire-and-rag bird costume and the placement of the "wildcat of culture" display next to a loudspeaker resonate with this practice of configuring taxonomically incongruent but poetically associative "visual bridges" (Bredekamp 1995, 73).

Neither the Kunstkammer nor the Lopes and Calixto spaces represent merely a bizarre collection of oddities in a disordered pseudo- or proto-museum. Instead, I see both as comprehensive attempts to visually represent an imagined cosmos unfolding through time, centered around a family depicted as powerful, noble, and reigning (literally or figuratively) over a given territory.

Although the Lopes and Calixto museum spaces suggest similar forward-looking desires, the groups were not equally well positioned to garner recognition through the process of *fazendo cultura*. The Lopes family's vehement claims to the crown of Arcoverde's *samba de coco* tradition surfaced in reaction to the increasing notoriety of Coco Raízes following Lula Calixto's death, as an attempt to set the record straight regarding the family's longer history of formally staging *samba de coco* performances. But while the appearance of tradition was essential to these groups' success in the early 2000s, proof of lineage was ultimately less important than performative factors, including stage presence, a photogenic look, and a sound that matched (or even surpassed) the intensity and energy level of most pop music performances. This litmus test of performance signaled a different winner than that of proof of lineage, and Coco Raízes's upward trajectory, toward larger and larger festival stages, attested to their ability to adjust their performances to different venues.

CHAPTER THREE

Nostalgia and Apocalypse

The Lopes and Calixto museums assembled artifacts to present particular family histories. The two families asserted claims to a musical heritage that, they hoped, would thrust them into a future of social recognition and fame. They were *fazendo cultura*—making culture, or making themselves cultural, thrusting themselves into the public sphere. They used the past to argue in the present in order to create a future, performing origins within a restorative nostalgic mode. Through their performances and exhibitions, they contributed to local efforts to rewrite Arcoverde's history, highlighting previously disavowed Afro-Brazilian contributions to the interior outpost. The mayor's office chose them as cultural emblems of a new Arcoverde, and they themselves chose to become cultural entrepreneurs, profiting from the new influx of visitors seeking the sources of Cordel's sounds.

At the same time, Cordel questioned the posture of homage expected within a folkloric register of cultural rescue, with its prescribed roles of rescuer and rescued. But while the band attempted to reject sanitized, restorative nostalgia and to refuse the strictures of folklore, it did not reject *samba de coco* outright. Instead, the members of Cordel simply broadened their vision beyond their initial sources of inspiration, drawing from several artistic reserves and deftly positioning themselves within several genres of cultural production. Their work entered into conversation with musicians of the region, but also came to engage with the Recife-based *mangue beat* pop music scene, Música Popular Brasileira (MPB), and the apocalyptic sounds of death metal. Beyond the sphere of music, they also took cues from poets, the revolutionary theater of Brecht and Artaud, 1960s avant-garde Cinema Novo, and filmmakers a generation later in the 1990s who reworked Cinema Novo themes. As a result their work became a genre-bending, critical reappraisal of previous efforts to portray their region as a territory of poverty. As the members of Cordel rethought how to represent their region, they positioned themselves within all three of the principal avenues of canonic validation that Ochoa outlines: national music, youth music, and the avant-garde (2006, 806).

It is tempting to understand this story as one in which Coco Raízes wrapped themselves in tradition, while Cordel rejected it. But upon closer scrutiny this opposition breaks down. Coco Raizes's performance is in some ways novel, and Cordel's performance remains in some ways rooted in place. Coco Raízes's inclusion in the São João Festival of harvest and homecoming was made novel by the fact that Afro-Brazilians were following it in the *sertão*. Cordel reconceived cultural rescue and its focus on roots, yet the band's songs remained stubbornly anchored in Arcoverde.

Looping Authentic Sounds: The Recordings of Coco Raízes

In April 2000 a van paid for by the municipality drove the newly formed Coco Raízes to Recife to record their first CD. The studio session began on the same day that the Lopes sisters were purposely left behind. The resulting recording reveals a tension between the Calixto and Gomes families' understanding of their music, on the one hand, and the discourses of roots within which audiences received their project, on the other. As Cordel began to explore allegorical terrain and an apocalyptic mood, audiences received Coco Raízes as a performance of heritage outside of commerce. Fans of Coco Raízes and even their managers from Recife described them as a "group" rather than a "band," explaining that this meant that the families should stay home rather than travel, so as not to lose their cultural identities.

Despite this pressure from without, Coco Raízes's recordings reveal the same sort of pride and ambition in *fazendo cultura* that the Lopes Museum displayed. The desire to belong to a broader cosmopolitan public sphere can be heard in the sound and the lyrics of the recordings. The families clearly assert themselves as cultural entrepreneurs and refuse to see themselves as outside of modernity and commerce. Their sense of home is complicated by narratives of migration that are blurred and submerged by the rapid-fire rhythms and rhymes.

In contrast to an aesthetics of liveness in which the same section is never played exactly the same way twice, listening closely to Coco Raízes records reveals a percussive, minimalist, multitracked sound with much in common with post-*mangue* artist and producer DJ Dolores. Granted, the sounds on Coco Raízes's recordings are all voices and percussion, unlike those of DJ Dolores, who trades in electronic bleeps and bloops mixed together with recordings of live instruments. In a Coco Raízes recording there are no purely synthesized or computer-generated sounds. Yet once digitally recorded, all sounds are subject to the same possibilities for cutting, pasting, manipulating, and looping. It sounds as if the recording engineer was pleased that he or she could save time by not having to record percussion parts for all twelve songs. Instead, the engineer appears to have recorded each instrument, including the dancers' feet, in one 3+3+2 *samba de coco* rhythm and one duple marchlike *foguete de roda* rhythm. The variation from song to song of the rhythmic background results not from different parts being played by the percussionists, but by the postproduction decisions of when to insert a given combination of instruments and when to mute them; when to speed them up electronically and when to slow them down; and when to loop the steadiest, tastiest 1–2 measure sections. The vocals are similarly looped. In many songs the tightest iterations of brief refrains sung by backing vocalists are chosen, copied, and pasted, so that the repetition of the refrain is identical. In certain songs even the lead vocals are repeated exactly through cutting and pasting, including idiosyncratic slides and stumbles replicated with machine precision. The use of autotune pitch correction, which blossomed into a well-known aesthetic choice in the pop music of the 2000s, was just starting to become standard practice. Slight warbles in the vocal formant of the singers suggest that this type of processing was being subtly applied in the studio on both their 2000 and 2002 records. By carefully applying this sonic touching-up, a certain measured amount of vocal out-of-tune-ness was deliberately left in to prevent a sound that is too polished—an engineered sound that would risk turning them from a group into a band.

One of the boldest production choices, I believe, is the use of time and pitch shifting, so that even the midtempo *coco* lullaby "Acorda Criança" ("Wake Up, Child") features the exact same tight percussion loop as much faster tracks on the CD. And although the technology to change the tempo without changing the pitch or vice versa was available in computer-based digital audio workstations in the early 2000s, the percussion loop used on the record changed pitch as it changed tempo throughout the record. This choice makes the percussion sound like a tape recording that is being slowed down or sped up from track to track. As I listen to the CD, I imagine the percussion instruments somehow growing or shrinking in the hands of the players, my mind accounting for the changes in pitch and timbral richness that accompany the changes in tempo. It is disorienting, tweaking the perception of balance in my inner ear.

Sense of place in the 2000 recording is unsettled and migratory in a way that belies the role of *samba de coco* as a representative of the cultural origins of a specific locale. One track sings of the life of the cowherder in the *sertão*, and another dreams about the coast, swaying in the surf in a dinghy. One of the standout tracks is the autobiographical Ciço Gomes tune "A Vida Tava Tão Boa" ("Life Used to Be So Good"), which in just a few couplets outlines how his life changed when his mother died when he was thirteen, forcing him to move between several different towns, staying with relatives and finding work. Songs marked public domain are featured alongside songs attributed to members of the group, some whose authorship is more controversial than others. One song was written by Antonio Xukuru, a member of the Xukuru nation who performed nearby with his own *coco* group. Agriculture, cattle ranching, migrant labor, coastal fishing, land disputes, and indigenous life are all referred to in the tracks.

The subsequent recording from 2002 broadens the list of geographical references and maintains the subtext of wanting to go elsewhere for love, money, friendship, social recognition, or all of the above. While Gomes sings on the first record that he plans to "Go to the South to make money," by the second record the spatial imagination of the group extends to several parts of the region. There are references to lands as far away as South Korea, a co-host of the 2002 World Cup soccer tournament. Many of the songs center on the pain and pleasure of traveling, most often by necessity for work, but also by choice as part of the life of the performer. They tell of going to the middle of the *sertão*; coastal Recife and its outskirts; cities surrounding Arcoverde in all directions; and other states such as nearby Sergipe, Maranhão closer to Amazonia, and Paraná in the South. No less than five kinds of birds, one honeybee, and a plane are featured in their songs, most often flying away, not unlike the miniature hot-air balloon in the Lopes Museum.

Near the end of the first CD, the lullaby "Acorda Criança" (Wake up, child) establishes a folkloric register of innocence through its lyrics, soothing melody, and backstory. According to Iram Calixto, she and Lula sat up the night before he died and wrote the song together. Unlike all of the other *cocos* the group has recorded, "Wake Up, Child" has a hymnlike quality to it. It is set at a slower tempo than all of the group's other songs, and its melody downplays the asymmetrical rhythmic timeline of the percussion. Notes are sustained throughout, and unlike on the rest of the CD, there is no rapid-fire, staccato *embolada* section or inclusion of the looped sounds of dancing sandals. The words tell of the innocent love between mother and child—the comfort and shelter found in her arms. This track became one of the group's most requested and popular songs.

If "Wake Up, Child" expresses an innocent intimacy focused inward toward family, the last two tracks on the second CD express a desire to push outward to public recognition. "Aperto de Mão" (Handshake) includes verses such as the following:

I left Arcoverde
I went to Recife
and after that to Sergipe
on the same plane

But later I returned
I went to the *sertão*
I have my luggage packed
I'm going to Maranhão

Eu saí de Arcoverde
Fui para Recife
Depois pra Sergipe
No mesmo avião

Mas depois eu voltei
Fui para o sertão
Tô de mala pronta
Vou pro Maranhão

"Não Brinco Mais" ("I'm Not Playing Anymore") includes these words:

I sang in Juazeiro
I sang in Ceará
I sang in Arcoverde
in Recife I came to play

If I were rich
I would earn lots of money
I would build a mansion
And have women to love
But since I can't
I'm leaving here in the North
And I'll only return to the North
When things get better

I sang with Cordel
With Cordel I came to sing
I sang with Lula Calixto
To make the party happen

Eu cantei no Juazeiro
Eu cantei no Ceará
Eu cantei em Arcoverde
No Recife vim brincar

Se eu fosse rico
Ganhasse muito dinheiro
Fazia uma mansão
De mulher pra namorar
Como eu não posso
Vou sair daqui do norte
Só volto daqui pro norte
Quando as coisas melhorar

Eu cantei com o Cordel
Com o Cordel eu vim cantar
Cantei com Lula Calixto
Pra festa nos animar

An Emblem of Roots, an Emblem of the Primitive

As audiences began to see Coco Raízes as Arcoverde's heritage, there was a tension present in the group's efforts to professionalize. On the one hand, the group was held up as an example of the essence of the region and a glimpse into its history. On the other hand, access to festival stages and recording studios led to significant shifts in the repertoire of Coco Raízes and how the musicians decided to present themselves. They calibrated their old-fashionedness, evoking the past according to contemporary production values. The following vignettes of live and recorded performances of Coco Raízes illustrate how their music accrued new meanings and uses as the sounds moved away from the *sertão*.

PROFESSIONALS ON STAGE: THE SÃO JOÃO FESTIVAL, ARCOVERDE, 2003

In a video taken at the 2003 São João Festival, Coco Raízes are playing on a small stage flanked with leaves. Their name is painted on a banner behind them, as is a large portrait of Lula Calixto. Unlike earlier staged performances, in which the musicians are obscured by a stage full of dancers, here they are visible. Ciço Gomes is singing to the crowd at the front of the stage, and three female singers (Iram, Iuma, and Dona Lourdes) stand behind him, performing synchronized movements at their microphone stands, like Motown background vocalists. The wholesale transfer of all the dancers from the street to the stage found in earlier performances has been replaced with a rotating system of two or three dancers on stage at a time. The Calixtos would soon consider it unprofessional to have the number of people on stage that they did at their first shows, teasing other local folkloric groups for maintaining so many members.

During the majority of the performance on the video, teenagers Fagner Gomes and Daiane Calixto are the only dancers on stage. They play to the crowd skillfully, demonstrating the dance steps, inventing choreography, and goofing around with each other. In addition to doing the slower *parcela* and quicker *trupé* steps, they hold hands and perform variations, some of which resemble swing dance moves. They move close together. They take three steps to the right and pivot. They take three steps to the left and pivot. Dancing the *trupé*, they stop cleanly on the same beat as the end of the *embolada* section. Daiane's old-fashioned skirt has three layers of ruffles that fan out independently as she spins.

The pitch and blend of the background harmony vocals are significantly tighter than they were before. The young dancers come down from the stage and stir up the energy of the crowd, grasping the hand of an audience member and leading the entire crowd in a spiral version of the *foguete de roda* round dance that was danced in a circle at the 1996 birthday party. Ciço leads the refrain "I'm going to the South, I'm going to make money" while the rest of the group, and much of the audience, sings the response.

TRADITION TO RESCUE OR POP TO CONSUME: CARNAVAL IN RECIFE, 2004

During the 2004 Carnaval in Pernambuco's capital, Coco Raízes performed twice in contrasting contexts that, taken together, indicated how the group was perched at the time between folklore managed with a paternalistic hand by the state and pop music competing in the musical marketplace. At its first performance it shared the bill with various other folkloric groups. The show took place in downtown Recife at the Pátio de São Pedro, a square leading to a colonial-era Catholic church. The plaza was lined with colonial architecture, and if audience members in jeans with piercings on their faces had not been in my field of vision, I could have pretended that I had been transported centuries into the past. That is, except for a strategically placed piece of graffiti high up on a wall next to the church, which pricked this fantasy. It was a grotesque, toadlike figure spray painted by soon-to-be famous graffiti artists Os Gêmeos, shrugging its shoulders and asking: "The question I ask myself is, am I art?"[1] When I had visited the square before, I had always admired the way that it so cleverly stripped the square's patina and placed the viewer firmly back in the present. This time, however, during carnaval, there was an enormous, expensive-looking circular decoration fashioned out of bolts of scarlet cloth propped up on the roof of an adjoining building to cover up the mischievous toad-troll. The decoration would have looked strangely out of place to anyone who didn't know what it was hiding.

Before Coco Raízes performed, there was an exhibition of folkloric dramatic dances. A representative of Recife's municipal government stood alone on stage, speaking into the microphone with a radio DJ's polished baritone. His job seemed to be to introduce the groups, then thank them in order to make them stop after the allotted number of minutes, even if they were in the middle of a song. The stage, like all 2004 Recife Carnaval stages, displayed the government's logo: a hand-drawn bridge with the slogan: "Our greatest work is to take care of the people." Whenever the announcer had a few seconds between acts, he would remind the audience that the carnaval was sponsored by the municipal government.

Each amateur group performing during the time slot preceding Coco Raízes was given seven minutes, and officials shooed some participants off the cobblestones when they dared to insist on finishing their songs. The speed of the changeover from one group to the next made microphone placement haphazard, so voices and instruments were often either too loud or inaudible. The groups were semichoreographed and delightfully visually chaotic until the announcer up on stage would interrupt, repeating into the microphone, "Thank you for participating! A round of applause for . . ." The enforced time limit, combined with the announcer's booming voice, drained the life out of these amateur performances. I imagined that earlier *samba de coco* performances were regulated like this. Some kept playing and singing even while the announcer was thanking them, countering the feeling that the performances were being managed, or even domesticated. Those moments, however, were brief, and ultimately led to acquiescence.

When it was finally time for Coco Raízes to play, Ciço walked on stage, wrested the microphone from the announcer with a smile, and commanded the crowd to move in closer. Immediately the previously apathetic crowd was caught up in stomping the steps of the *coco*.

Their second performance during carnaval was on a much larger Rec-Beat stage and produced by Cordel's manager Gutie, featuring a mixture of traditional groups and pop bands. A small plywood platform with a microphone placed near Fagner and Daiane's feet amplified the sounds of their stomping. Sections of songs were choreographed to showcase the quick steps of their *trupé*. The percussion would stop, and their thundering feet would sustain the precise rhythmic groove for eight measures before coming back in. They performed a new song about a train that accelerated in tempo, pushing the dancers to their limits to whip up the crowd's energy.[2]

The urban audience loved it. Coco Raízes's performance was the only Rec-Beat show to receive an encore in four days of carnaval. After finishing, obviously exhilarated, they threw their hats and wooden sandals into the crowd like rock stars, and offstage they were promptly surrounded by press from Rio de Janeiro and São Paulo.

LOCAL SOUNDS: CHAMBER OF COMMERCE FAIR

The recorded music of Coco Raízes provided the soundtrack to the local chamber of commerce convention in Arcoverde in 2004, further confirming their status as the city's representative of popular culture. I realized immediately that I was underdressed in an untucked T-shirt and jeans. The crowd represented the elite of Arcoverde, with the exception of stiltwalking clowns perilously distributing flyers in the narrow aisles between rows of booths. The convention was spotless; the booths were shiny and professional. The SESC had a presence there, as did several local banks. There was a booth with a fully functioning hair salon and an anti-abortion display featuring human fetuses in jars floating in formaldehyde. The loudspeakers blasted Coco Raízes singing "I'm going to the South, I'm going to make money" as a stiltwalker towered above the conventioneers, mouthing the lyrics and dancing *coco*.

TRIBAL SOUNDS IN A SHOPPING MALL

The Paço Alfandega is a high-end shopping mall in a remodeled warehouse in the restored colonial district of Recife. The mall features exposed brick, large wooden beams, and a glass elevator visible from the four-story atrium. In equal tribute to local iconoclasts and traditionalists, the third floor is named after *mangue beat* founder Chico Science, and the second floor is named after novelist, playwright, and noted traditionalist Ariano Suassuna. Fashionistas clad in black were seated on three sides of the atrium—on the fourth side stood the glass elevator. Directly facing the elevator was a slightly raised press platform where a gaggle of photographers and television camera operators crouched, waiting for the chic fashion show to begin. I found a perch halfway up the stairway on one of the sides next to an escalator. The models entered the glass elevator on the top floor and froze into their mannequin poses before descending to the catwalk below. As the elevator began to descend, the Coco Raízes track "Godê Pavão" played over the loudspeakers. Iram's voice echoed lyrics about long, pleated skirts while a model with blue-black skin and a shaved head strutted out of the glass elevator and onto the catwalk, her breasts exposed except for some vaguely "African" rings gathered around her neck and chest. The models who came after her almost all appeared to be white to light-skinned *mestiço*, except for one who had dark skin and a teased, exaggerated Afro hairdo. They were all painted in splotches of black, mostly on their faces, although one had an exposed breast painted inky black, like the body painting of certain Brazilian indigenous groups. The music shifted to an insistent dance beat with layers of polyrhythmic hand drums and a string quartet playing a short repeating pattern.

After the fashion show, DJ Dolores told me that the organizers of the show had asked him to spin something "tribal."

As these vignettes suggest, Coco Raízes had become the emblematic traditional group touted in Arcoverde's promotion of tourism. The group had gained access to prominent venues for live performance. Its recordings were used to celebrate Arcoverde's commercial sector and to add "tribal" spice to a chic fashion show in Recife. The chamber of commerce convention used Coco Raízes to brand and bolster the cultural distinctiveness of Arcoverde. The fashion show, in contrast, used *samba de coco* as an allegorical soundtrack indexing the African ingredient of Brazilian identity, conflated with a sign of the primitive or tribal to be juxtaposed with haute couture fashions and string quartets.

Coco Raízes consciously shifted from performing a participatory form to performing a presentational form as the group began performing for larger audiences. Nevertheless, the dancers continued to emphasize the participatory on stage, downplaying the gap between audience and performers. The dancing style became more standardized, as Fagner and Daiane became the models that other dancers and audience members emulated. Wooden sandals on resonant plywood platforms captured by microphones allowed them to project the sounds of the steps and incorporate them into the songs as another layer of percussion. The mass of dancers was pared down to two or three representatives who demonstrated the steps and encouraged the audience to join in. The virtuoso steps, which had become even more challenging as tempos accelerated, were showcased as heroic feats performed by experts.

Coco Raízes strove to balance the performance of roots and locality with contemporary production values with a broadly consumable sound. Inevitably, some fans feared that the group would become too slick or *estilizado* as they professionalized. For them, Coco Raízes's distance from modernity, whether spatial (living away from the capital and closer to rural life) or temporal (keeping heritage alive), was part of their appeal.

Bridging Desert and Swamp: Cordel and Mangue Beat

When Cordel arrived in Recife in 1999, its members positioned themselves in relation to the new music scene in the city. The coastal capital is where the novel stylistic combinations known as *mangue beat*, and the rejuvenated explorations of musical roots known as *música de raíz*, had emerged in the early to mid-1990s. Cordel's challenge was to stage a performance that resonated with and engaged in a dialogue with *mangue beat* and *música de raíz* without falling prey to being labeled merely imitators of their coastal counterparts.[3]

Mangue beat, like *tropicalismo* a generation earlier, brought together national music and youth music with a grand inaugural gesture complete with an accompanying manifesto. The founders of *mangue beat*—Chico Science and his friends Fred 04 and journalist Renato L—developed a manifesto in response to the finding of a Washington, D.C., nonprofit claiming that Recife was one of the five worst places on Earth to live. In the manifesto they describe the *mangue*, or mangrove swamp upon which Recife is built, as an ecosystem whose ugliness obscures its valuable biodiversity. The two bands that founded the scene, Chico Science e a Nação Zumbi and Mundo Livre S/A, entangled contemporary global popular music such as punk rock, heavy metal, funk, and hip-hop with Afro-Pernambucan genres like *coco* and *maracatu*, as well as the samba-funk of Rio de Janeiro–based Jorge Ben.

Cordel sought to distinguish itself from the narrow definition of *mangue beat* and yet remain within its orbit in order to win over its fans and offer a kind of response to the coastal scene from the interior of the state. To this end, Lirinha rejected being labeled *mangue beat*, but conceded that the band fit within the diverse *mangue* "swamps." To distinguish themselves in Recife, the band members emphasized their hometown roots and stressed Arcoverde's distance from the coastal capital and its proximity to the *sertão*. They used their origins to produce a performance that matched the intensity of Chico Science, while introducing a distinct local reserve of musical traditions and poetry from the Pernambucan *sertão*.

Cordel adopted many of the stances and stylistic elements of *mangue beat*, while in effect critiquing it from the rural margins. For example, in the first track on the seminal debut *Da lama ao caos* (From mud to chaos), Chico Science chants with a prophetic declamatory voice inspired by his idol Chuck D from the radical U.S. political hip-hop group Public Enemy. During his speech he pays homage to rebellious figures in the history of the Americas, such as Zapata and Sandino. Chico Science pairs these political revolutionaries and heroes of the Latin American Left with northeastern Brazilian legends Zumbi dos Palmares, who led a colony of escaped slaves, and Lampião, a charismatic early twentieth-century outlaw from the *sertão*. Chico Science also name-checks Antonio Conselheiro, a maverick Catholic millenarian preacher who attempted to build a utopian community in the *sertão* at the end of the nineteenth century, only to see it decimated by government troops. The *mangue beat* pioneer famously yelled, "Fear of origins is a bad thing!," offering an alternative canon of rebellious figures, including northeasterners who were killed by the government.

Despite Chico Science's declared return to origins, *mangue beat*'s gestures toward tradition were highly filtered through contemporary global trends in popular music. Lirinha took up the mantle of Chico Science's prophetic register, but distanced it from its U.S. hip-hop model, using his rural accent and delivery honed at cowboy poetry recitation contests to assert that he could more ably embody the *sertão* rebels Conselheiro and Lampião. In addition, the presence of Emerson Calado in the band, with his Xukuru family roots, and the embattled Xukuru territory being located so near Arcoverde, led Cordel to further multiculturalize this band of prophets. In its lyrics the band cited indigenous prophecies and examples of rebellion alongside the incantations of Luso- and Afro-Pernambucan heroes.

Cordel was asserting, in effect, that while Chico Science sang that fear of origins is a bad thing, his urban, coastal existence precluded him from truly growing up with these origins. Within the antipurist *mangue* realm of tradition gleefully "poisoned" by novel sonic recombinations, Cordel offered new reserves of melodies, genres, and poetry to be recombined, claiming closer proximity to the cultural wellspring. The band added two drummers from the Recife slum of Morro da Conceição who had grown up playing in Afro-Brazilian *candomblé*/Xangô religious communities. By adding Afro-Brazilian sounds from Recife, the group sought to represent the *sertão* and the *favela* as shared territories of poverty and social margins, rather than as opposed Luso- and Afro-Brazilian cultural and musical fields, as the two zones are often heard and understood.

Chico Science was a technophile; even his day job at a government agency involved computers. He and his friends first named *mangue beat* *mangue bit*, to juxtapose the mangrove swamp with the computer bit, celebrating the coming of the Internet as the opening of information flows coincided with the promise of political opening in the 1990s. In contrast, Cordel's use of new musical technologies was more muted. While Chico Science played with samples and loops, hip-hop style, and talked about the "organic sampler" of their rhythm section that recombined traditional maracatu beats, Cordel used samples as sound effects to establish setting. For example, a representative Cordel sample was the sound of thunder and rain triggered from backstage that accompanied "Tempestade (A Dança do Trovão)" (Tempest [dance of the thunder]), an elemental shout to the heavens as a storm erupts. Cordel was also more stubborn in avoiding electric guitars and electric basses in the ensemble, integrating Clayton's fingerpicked nylon-string acoustic guitar with the three percussionists' formidable wall of sound. Cordel was determined to match or surpass the volume and intensity of punk rock, metal, and *mangue beat*, without using rock instrumentation. The band positioned itself as not quite roots music, not quite heavy metal, and not quite *mangue beat*, but able to share a festival stage with performances of any of the three.

Genres that fly the banner of musical hybridity rely on the fixity of traditional genres so that the sonic ingredients remain identifiable within their novel mixtures. Cordel's move to differentiate its songs from earlier mutationist popular music, such as *tropicália* and *mangue beat*, involved a shift in the mode of quotation—the precise way in which other genres were digested within the new form. Cordel attempted to embody the Pernambucan interior of notorious bandits and preachers with greater historical depth and detail than urban, coastal Chico Science could convincingly do. Compared with *mangue beat*, Cordel drained the giddiness out of its mode of quotation. It deflated the techno-optimistic pop sensibility of *mangue beat* in the service of lessening the distance between the mutationist doing the quoting and the culture bearers being marked and quoted.

Between the Allegorical and the Visceral: Cordel, MPB, and Heavy Metal

To understand why 1990s *mangue beat* (and by extension, Cordel) was such a significant development in the recent history of Brazilian popular music, it is productive to turn back to the 1980s, when Micheliny and Lirinha grew up in a time and a place they considered "without history, without memory, and without culture." This feeling wasn't unique to them or to Arcoverde. The rock soundtrack of the 1980s often describes the decade of the Brazilian dictatorship's slow transition to democracy as a time and place without memory.

When Chico Science called for a return to origins, despite the fact that his sound was primarily cosmopolitan and global, he was intervening at a specific moment in the recent history of popular music in Brazil. Idelber Avelar clarifies the rift between national music and youth music that preceded the *mangue* shift in his insightful essay comparing Milton Nascimento and Sepultura in the 1980s during the political opening in the last years of military rule (Perrone and Dunn 2001, 123–135). Sepultura and Milton Nascimento, both from the state of Minas Gerais, represent the rift between MPB and heavy metal that was later bridged by Cordel in the late 1990s. While Milton Nascimento and early-career Sepultura represented a cultural chasm, Cordel drew from both bodies of work.

In comparing Milton Nascimento and Sepultura, Avelar focuses principally on the chronotopes of MPB and death metal, examining the genres' violently contrasting temporalities and distinct senses of place. Milton traded in melancholic tales of loss and mournful rituals of migration from the interior to the city. Sepultura and other Brazilian death metal bands, in contrast, raged within an apocalyptic, end-time temporality, treating home as a dissolute and suicidal place—a place only to be abandoned. Milton reappropriated Catholic messages of charity and fraternity and deployed them, in the context of the dictatorship, to nourish hopes of popular political emancipation. Sepultura inverted crosses and made satanic allusions in an effort to negate this hope that "underneath the conservative, conventional, traditional, and religious universe of Minas Gerais resided some emancipatory, fraternal and compassionate kernal politically and culturally available" (Perrone and Dunn 2001, 129). Death metal is music of radical negation fueled by frustration, pessimism, and despair in the face of living in the heart of a modern, industrialized zone but being excluded from its fruits.

These contrasts are embedded in the musical vocabularies of the two groups. Milton is known for his exquisite voice and his long, stretched-out notes that ache with melancholy. His songs often sound within the reverberating acoustic space of colonial-era Catholic churches in Minas Gerais. Death metal, on the other hand, features powerful, grim, jackhammer-like repetition and lockstep, machine-gun-like rhythms that seek to obliterate the breathing room necessary to reflect, remember, and mourn. While the MPB of Milton spins oblique discursive allegories of violence in beautiful, sophisticated, melodic compositions, Sepultura's death metal—and much Brazilian rock more broadly—viscerally enacts the social violence of a life alienated from politics, where dreams of upward mobility die amid the erosion of the middle class.

A decade later, in the 1990s, *mangue beat* contributed to reopening an engagement between these estranged musical and lyrical reserves: MPB and rock, or more broadly, national music and youth music. Cordel entered this musical flow inaugurated by Chico Science by carefully integrating national and regional themes with the negative aesthetics of heavy metal. In particular, they played with death metal's apocalyptic temporality and forceful negation of place in an effort to undercut celebratory, restorative national-cultural nostalgia. To clarify how the band positioned itself within the shifting genre boundaries of *mangue beat*, MPB, and rock, I read certain key

Cordel tracks here, starting with the two "prophecies" from its first recording: "Profecia (ou Testamento da Ira)"(Prophecy [or testament of ire]), which helps open the CD, and "Profecia Final (ou No Mais Profundo)" (Final prophecy [or in the deepest]), which helps close it.

"Prophecy (or Testament of Ire)" begins with the declaration of solidarity "Long live the Xukuru people!," highlighting the band's proximity to the contemporary struggle for land of an indigenous group that lives near Arcoverde. Emerson Calado, the principal drummer of the group, is a Xukuru descendant. This invocation multiculturalizes the prophetic register, drawing not just from ecstatic, elemental aspects of Luso-Brazilian Catholicism, but also from local indigenous belief and Afro-Brazilian possession-based religious rites. It also reminds the listener that violent national struggles often relegated to the past are still being waged in the present. Only a few months before Cordel's first performance in 1998, Xukuru chief Chicão was assassinated after the courts ratified indigenous land claims and required Luso-Brazilian and *mestiço* landowners to return lands to the indigenous group. The first lines quote the prophecy of early twentieth-century indigenous shaman Pajé Cauã, who claimed; "A new era will begin with two braided snakes / Drought and blood." Lirinha continues:

> Heirs to the new millennium
> There is no longer any doubt
> The desert will become the sea
> And the sea, yes
> After flooding the narrowest of paths
> Will become the desert
>
> Antôe [Antonio Conselheiro] was right, my faithful flock
>
> The land belongs to everyone
> The land belongs to no one
>
> . . .
>
> Children of the crucible
> Heirs to the end of the world
> Burn your story so badly told

Expanding on Chico Science's mention of Conselheiro in his speech inaugurating *mangue beat*, Lirinha deepens this tribute to the maverick millenarian preacher by intoning Conselheiro's pronouncement of impending radical change. By stating that the land belongs to everyone and no one, Lirinha invokes the allegorical role of the *sertão* in literature and 1960s Cinema Novo as a place of rebellion where revolution was most likely to be sparked. What is interesting here, in the context of the 1980s rift between the temporalities of MPB and death metal, is the way in which Cordel flirts with an apocalyptic temporality, while refusing to blot out all Milton Nascimento–style expressions of hope. The line "Heirs to the new millennium" suggests a forward gaze into the future, where hope for radical change flickers. The later line "Heirs to the end of the world / Burn your story so badly told," recited with revival tent fervor, borrows from an apocalyptic mood without focusing on an imagined end-day scenario. The supposed end days have already come and gone, the track implies, suggesting that the time has come to find other ways to narrate their region. Rather than setting their performance in the "no-place" of death metal that eclipses nostalgia, Cordel borrows and localizes an apocalyptic affect. This allows the band to access local musical and poetic reserves and to creatively mine moments in regional history that resonate with the alternative canon of rebellious figures that the group invokes and embodies.

In one of the final tracks on the first recording, "Final Prophecy (or In the Deepest)," Lirinha quotes the notorious bandit Lampião to send a message to the Recife scene. In the original letter that Lampião sent to the governor of Pernambuco in 1926, the outlaw stakes out his territory with bluster, declaring the interior of the state to be a place where government troops pursue him at their own peril. He establishes the place of Arcoverde, then called Rio Branco, as the dividing line between the *agreste* region that approaches the coast and the interior *sertão* region. Cordel's use of this quotation boasts its access to a reserve of interior styles less known in the capital that distinguish Cordel's sound from *mangue beat*:

> I am governing this zone, from here all the way until
> The point where the trails meet in Rio Branco [Arcoverde]
> And you, sir, govern your part, from Rio Branco until the edge of the sea

Two other songs from Cordel's repertoire, "Cio da Terra" (Fecundity of the earth) and "Vou Saquear a Tua Feira" (I'm going to loot your market), demonstrate the reopening of dialogue between national music and youth music, while also bearing the influence of revolutionary drama more theorized in theater and cinema. As Cordel moved away from a preservationist approach, it positioned itself within multiple, overlapping genres of cultural production.

"Fecundity of the Earth" speaks most directly to bridging the rift between MPB and metal. A cover of a song by iconic MPB artists Milton Nascimento and Chico Buarque that Cordel often performed but never recorded, "Fecundity of the Earth" idealizes the cycles of agricultural production, from harvesting wheat and cane to devouring delicious bread and cane juice. In the duet between Milton Nascimento and Chico Buarque, fragile, melancholy harmonies resonate with the style of the brotherly duos of *música caipira*, who lament the loss of rural lifestyles as so many move to the city. But like many of Milton Nascimento's compositions, the harmonies of the guitar accompaniment reach even further back than *música caipira*, harboring a whiff of colonial-era church music. The appearance of the song in the documentary *The Spirit of Samba* reinforces the interpretation of "Cio da Terra" as a melancholy lament. In the film a sober, reserved Milton and Chico sing the song live, while the filmmakers intersperse footage of the singers with affecting shots of miserable urban poverty. Milton and Chico's version is about memory, loss, mourning, and social critique, pitched in the form of a prayer to the earth.

Cordel's cover of Milton and Chico's song best illustrates how the band drew upon the poetic and musical reserves of both MPB and metal. The cover version of the song begins with a quiet, fingerpicked accompaniment that resembles the original. The vocals, however, are barked in staccato unison, unlike the tight, blended, and lyrical harmonies of Milton and Chico. As the song continues, it erupts into a heavy, distorted dirge. The irregular phrase lengths that contribute to the fragility of the original transform into the kinds of pounding, drum-fill-led phrases found in metal, and the harmonic accompaniment is injected with parallel fifths, taking the song out of the church and into the arena of a heavy metal show. Within this new arrangement a mournful posture is still retained, as Lirinha points in desperation to the ground as he sings about the harvest. But to him land is violently contested, sometimes drought-ridden, often to be abandoned and never available to all. Cordel's cover version of the song adds rage to the melancholy and complicates its mourning. The only formal change that the band made to Milton and Chico's arrangement is a carthartic bellow heard after the verses. It is a shout that occupies a space between Milton's stretching of time and the carnal cries of anguish more commonly found in metal. When I asked the drummer Emerson Calado about the argument that Cordel merged these previously separate vocabularies, he responded matter of factly. "There are members of the band like Clayton who are fans of Milton," he explained, "and members of the band like me who are fans of metal."

"Vou Saquear a Tua Feira" (I'm going to loot your market) is another key example of Cordel's combination of Milton and metal. On the track a distanced, dialectical approach to addressing underlying reasons for the persistent poverty in the region coexists with a visceral enactment of looting and violence. The song was inspired by newspaper headlines chronicling the rioting and looting of food by the hungry in the Pernambucan interior during periodic droughts. The track begins with the roar of an approaching mob. Glass breaks, screams are heard, horses stampede. In the chaos, a voice yells "The land belongs to no one!" and the drums and guitar lay down a stampede-like groove. The verses are sung/screamed by Lirinha and sung by the rest of the band as if they were participants in the riot.

The chorus, in contrast, is more removed from the pandemonium, with a gentle underlying 3/4 time signature and square, *reisado*-like melody mostly made up of quarter notes. Distanced from the mob, surveying the scene, the song sketches a dialectics of violence, attempting to move beyond a shortsighted view of the mob as simply criminals without regard for the social conditions leading to their outburst. Far from demonizing the rioters or pitying them for their poverty, the song unearths the issues surrounding the extreme social inequality that provide the soil that nourishes this conflict. When they sing of the *sertão* as "fallow land without an owner," using the colonial term *sesmaria*, they remind the listener of a time when the colonial government doled out plots of land to colonists after taking them from the indigenous groups of the area, thus identifying property ownership as part of the root cause of poverty.

The song can also be read in the context of the band asserting its particular, anarchic rethinking of northeastern folklore—the efforts of its members to burn the stories of their region that they considered so badly told. The market in question is one of the supermarkets looted in recent headlines, but it can also be imagined as the markets of tradition in places like nearby Caruaru, where quaint figurines of violent Lampião are sold while pipe and tabor bands wander among the stalls, charming tourists.

Smearing the Cosmetics of Hunger: Cordel and Brazilian Cinema

As Cordel distanced itself from the folkloric, it positioned itself within several overlapping genres. *Mangue beat* in Recife was a key scene with which it allied itself at the same time that it worked to distinguish itself from the groups that had come before it. The shifting genres of MPB and Brazilian rock provide a broader field within which the band struggled to position itself. During the same 1990s postauthoritarian moment in which dialogue had been reopened between MPB and rock, Brazilian filmmakers were revisiting the mythologized territories of poverty of the *sertão* and the *favela*. They grappled with and rethought the legacy of 1960s Cinema Novo from immediately before the national trauma of military rule. Cordel was also entangled in this process of reworking prior representations of the region through cinema. It positioned itself within and drew creatively from the 1990s cinematic "rediscovery" of the *sertão*.

In "Vou Saquear a Tua Feira" (I'm going to loot your market), Cordel alternates between enacting violent desperation spurred by chronic hunger and poverty and standing back to examine the root causes of persistent hunger and poverty. This movement within the song marks a revisiting of certain predictatorship aspects of 1960s Cinema Novo. In particular, it resonates with the aesthetics of hunger as outlined by the influential Brazilian Cinema Novo director Glauber Rocha. In the early 1960s Rocha was concerned with cinematic depictions of territories of poverty such as the *sertão* and the *favela*. In particular, he decried sentimental, humanist representations of these regions because, in his view, they failed to force audiences to experience the brutality of poverty and hunger. To Rocha the tears shed by audiences when they were moved by sentimental depictions of territories of poverty only served to distance them from the social violence that afflicts such regions.

Rocha's fiery anticolonial rhetoric did not preclude his drawing upon critical aesthetic thought from Europe, however. His sensibility as a filmmaker was informed by developments within the European avant-garde, including Bertolt Brecht and Antonin Artaud, two prominent dramatic theorists of revolutionary twentieth-century theater. "I'm Going to Loot Your Market" demonstrates the tension that exists between these Brechtian and Artaudian approaches. Placing the listener in the role of a rioter surrounded by violence and destruction resonates with Artaud's "Theatre of Cruelty," which aims to create an intense emotional experience in which the audience becomes so swept up in the performance that it strips away their social being. Cordel stopped short of seeking to strip away northeastern identity, however. The band was more interested in refanging the myths of its region than in completely stripping them away. The chorus of the song, which takes a step back and reminds the listener of the centuries-old root causes of poverty in the region, is more in line with Brecht's "Epic Theatre." Elaborating a Marxian approach to theater, Brecht sought to detach the audience member from the spectacle. His goal was to foster a critical viewer who would analyze the materialist dialectics underlying the events depicted on stage. To this end, Brecht even encouraged theatergoers to smoke during his shows, with the hope that this would help them to maintain their critical distance. Brechtian actors often attempted to convey not just their character, but also their awareness that they were acting, just as Cordel did when it pulled away from the hunger riot to comment on it.

Although both approaches were present in Cordel's simultaneously bruising and cerebral performances, the band's move from theatrical settings to music festivals contributed to the foregrounding of Artaudian spectacle over Brechtian dialectics. The form of a two- to five-minute pop song, as opposed to a plot-driven, three-hour play or film, is more conducive to the immediacy of reworking regional emblems than it is to a comprehensive diagnosis of social ills.

This isn't the first time in the history of Brazilian popular music that artists have drawn upon the critical aesthetics of Cinema Novo. In the late 1960s, during the most repressive days of the military dictatorship, Caetano Veloso cited the Glauber Rocha film *Entranced Earth* (1967; *Terra em Transe*) as the inspiration for the *tropicália* movement in its absurdist tendencies and pessimism toward politics. A generation later, Cordel positioned itself both inside and outside *mangue beat*, which was itself a scene being crowned as the heir to *tropicália*. In an effort to remain within the orbit of *mangue beat*, Cordel drew upon an earlier predictatorship Glauber Rocha film, *Black God, White Devil* (1964; *Deus e o Diabo na Terra do Sol*).

Black God, White Devil alternates between long, silent footage of the *sertão* during a drought and spasms of quick-cut footage of violence. It tells the story of a peasant who first places his hopes in a messianic religious leader and then in an outlaw bandit. Ultimately disillusioned with both charismatic leaders, he breaks free from older millenarian visions of social change and moves toward a secular, radical Left consciousness. The shocking Artaudian moments of violence and the Brechtian slow pans, meant to leave space for critical reflection, fuel Glauber Rocha's effort to make the audience feel the oppressive heat, hunger, and poverty, all the while contemplating how such an unbearable situation could be changed. Performing within the field of 1990s popular music rather than 1960s cinema, Cordel tapped into the power of the prophetic, millenarian register. The band members sought to, in their words, "jackhammer" the sedimented representations of their region and open space for more nuanced scripts to narrate the place of the Northeast within Brazil as a nation.

Cordel was not alone in revisiting 1960s Cinema Novo and its representations of territories of poverty. After the Collor administration sharply decreased funding for cinema in 1989, filmmaking largely ground to a halt until the mid-1990s, when then-president Fernando Henrique Cardoso restored funding, producing a burst of creativity that is now referred to as the *retomada*, or return. During the *retomada*, documentary and feature filmmakers alike set their projects in the social margins, especially the *sertão* and the *favela* (Nagib 2003, 97–104). But the ways in which they depicted these territories of poverty starkly contrasted with the productions of the radical wave of the 1960s. For example, the Oscar-nominated *Central do Brasil* (*Central Station*), one of the internationally successful films of the *re-*

tomada, pays homage to the *sertão* of Glauber Rocha. Its protagonists take a bus trip from a gritty Rio de Janeiro to a gentle, decent northeastern *sertão*. The same territory used as a setting in Rocha's *Deus e o Diabo* is covered, but rather than using the *sertão* allegorically as a land of rebellion, *Central do Brasil* presents it in a sentimental light, where salt-of-the-earth people with good hearts get by the best that they can. Footage of the destination of the film's road trip was shot down the road from Arcoverde. Severina Lopes was featured in a speaking role as a woman leading thousands of people in prayer at a pilgrimage site, and Lula Calixto performed his fife at the opening event held for the participants.

Film scholar Ivana Bentes describes *Central Station*'s "tourism through the Glauberian *sertão*" as a "cosmetics of hunger" to differentiate these reassuring images from the deliberately jarring "aesthetics of hunger" of Cinema Novo (Nagib 2003, 125). To Bentes, many films that follow the "cosmetics of hunger" use the *sertão* as a scruffy but charming backdrop rather than a territory of poverty and violence to be decried through its visceral depiction. By drawing on the harshness of the aesthetics of hunger, Cordel went against the grain of the prevailing cosmetics of hunger. The band rejected sentimental and celebratory regionalism and remained closer to the combination of Artaudian "Theatre of Cruelty" and Brechtian alienation effects found in early Cinema Novo. *Deus e o Diabo* serves as a template for Cordel, in that the film invokes mythologized, messianic figures Conselheiro and Lampião folded into Marxist ideology; it features a narrator inspired by *literatura de cordel*; and it includes folklore as an ingredient in the mix, but not one that should necessarily be trusted or privileged.

Courting the "Reader/Listener": Cordel, Literature, and Poetry

Micheliny Verunschk located Cordel's position on the cusp of the oral/aural and the written word when she wrote that the band "demands an ideal reader/listener that, supplied with knowledge of the literary and extraliterary world, can perceive their polyphony and become a co-author." She describes Lirinha's practice as "stylistic kleptomania," using intertextuality as a resource that "ferociously and in the tiniest detail cuts and stitches together poetic references."[4] Lirinha chose sources from century-old northeastern popular poetry and celebrated literary works to recent canonical and oral tradition poetry and prose. His broad range of source material contributed to the creation of the band's expansive temporality, drawing the reader/listener back to the time of the late nineteenth-century Canudos rebellion before oscillating back to the present.

Although the amount of spoken-word poetry shrank as Cordel the theatrical folklore revue became Cordel the band, moments were still set aside during performances for Lirinha to recite poetry. Two tracks, "Ai se sesse" (Oh, if it was) and "Dos três mal-amados" (Of three badly loved ones), serve as prominent examples of his use of popular and canonical poetry. "Dos três mal-amados" represents an Artaudian impulse to tear down false constructs such as the antiquated story of their region. "Ai se sesse," in contrast, is regional folk poetry that restores a measure of innocence to the proceedings. In this way the two poems represent the contrary pull of reflective nostalgia and restorative nostalgia within Cordel's work.

"Dos três mal-amados," on Cordel's second recording, is excerpted from a poem by the celebrated canonical poet João Cabral de Melo Neto. The poem is punctuated throughout with the echoing sounds of a sledgehammer demolishing a wall of concrete and ceramic tile, as well as other thunderous and crackling percussion: "O amor comeu meu nome, minha identidade, meu retrato. O amor comeu minha certidão de idade, minha genealogia, meu endereço." ("Love ate my name, my identity, my portrait. Love ate my identification card, my genealogy, my address.").

This theme of all-consuming passion dovetails with Artaud's desire to "turn against language and its basely utilitarian . . . sources, against its trapped-beast origins" (Brustein 1964, 374). The critic Robert Brustein explains Artaud's belief that words harbor the "diseases of civilization," precipitating a "dissipation of mystery" (ibid.). Yet Artaud does not turn away from words completely. Instead, he calls for a theater that uses language "rather for its emotional coloring and incantatory tone" (ibid.). This poem, with hypnotic repetition, intones a list of the rationalized, bureaucratic details of João Cabral do Melo Neto's conscious identity as the details become increasingly irrelevant in a flood of passion. Although the poet may have been referring to love between one individual and another, Cordel's performance of the poem, recited with demolition sound effects, places more weight on the numbers and concepts being devoured than on what is doing the devouring. In this way the band moves away from Brecht and toward Artaud—away from fostering cold, detached analysis and toward provoking ecstatic fervor.

In the unabridged version of the poem, Pernambucan João Cabral de Melo Neto wrote: "O amor comeu meu Estado e minha cidade. Drenou a água morta dos mangues, aboliu a maré." ("Love ate my state and my city. It drained the dead water of the mangrove swamps, abolished the tide."). This peeling away at the layers of the individual and social subject closely follows Artaud's dedication to "renouncing psychological man, with his well-dissected characters and feelings, and social man, submissive to laws and misshapen by religions and precepts" (Brustein 1964, 373). These lines, which most overtly deny nationalist/regionalist celebration or at least complicate it, were excised. In the original poem, the *mangue* was eaten along with everything else.

After the stormy, monstrous, and ghostly elements of their performances, Cordel ultimately returned to a register of innocence with the poem "Ai se sesse," chanted unaccompanied, in reverent tones, by Lirinha and the audience. The audience even has hand gestures that go along with the recitation. The band's first CD ends with a microphone recording of a portable stereo playing a cassette tape of a performance of this poem.[5] Lirinha introduces it like this: "We came from the Pernambucan *sertão* over there, a city called Arcoverde. Poet Zé da Luz from the turn of the century wrote a poem because they told him that in order to talk about love it was necessary to speak correct Portuguese and all." In the poem, the protagonist expresses the depth of his love for his romantic partner by pledging to cut open the underbelly of heaven with a knife if St. Peter gives her any trouble entering the pearly gates after she dies.

Written on the page, the poem risks being read as rural caricature, with ungrammatical lines such as "Se um dia nós se gostasse" ("If one day we was to love one another"). But the mood in the venue whenever I heard Lirinha recite "Ai se sesse" was both giddy and imbued with a churchlike reverence. After nearly every show, he faithfully invoked his Arcoverde roots before leaving the stage and led the young, well-educated audience in a ritual that allowed them to loudly affirm that pathos and illiteracy are not mutually exclusive. The poem's narrator fits São João art director Suedson Neiva's description of Lula Calixto: "His simplicity was his greatness." In the special features of the group's MTV-released DVD of a live performance, there are two separate takes of "Ai se sesse." In the first, Lirinha and the audience recite together; in the second, he simply speaks the first line and steps back, silent, in awe of the energy of the crowd's collective voice as fans chant the entire poem on a crescendo of enthusiasm. The emotional pitch of the moment reveals the audience's heartfelt investment in this populist message. At the same time, the protagonist's naïve devotion so poignantly delivered, with accentuated Pernambucan pronunciation, returns the performance to a register of innocence that offers closure for the band's detours into the apocalyptic.

As this chapter outlines, the careers of Coco Raízes and Cordel in the first half of the 2000s were entangled, yet their respective projects were distinct and occupied different genres. By 2004, even though the two groups sang about each other, they only occasionally came face to face. The members of Cordel were living in São Paulo by this point. They spent most of their days traveling throughout Brazil, playing show after show. Their relationship to their hometown in their music became more complicated, as their positioning within various genres of cultural production illustrates. Nevertheless, they established a tradition of returning each year to perform for the São João Festival and to visit their family and friends. São João became the only time each year that Cordel performed alongside Coco Raízes, Coco Irmãs Lopes, and the Reisado das Caraíbas, all groups that it cited as inspirations. Even though Lirinha and Clayton were closest to Lula Calixto, the band maintained contact with the rest of Coco Raízes after his death and often visited the Alto do Cruzeiro when they were in Arcoverde.

In the next chapters I focus on the months leading up to the annual São João Festival in 2004 and on the festival itself. I examine the filming and reception of a television documentary about *samba de coco* that was broadcast nationwide to celebrate the June festival and how the TV Globo network renders *samba de coco* within a lens of restorative nostalgia that blots out modernity. This depiction is contrasted with Cordel's attempts to rework this script in its own video productions, highlighting a cosmopolitan, contemporary regionalism.

CHAPTER FOUR

Television

When a journalist from TV Globo came to Arcoverde in the weeks leading up to the São João Festival in June 2004, the *samba de coco* families were excited by the prospect of being featured on television.[1] It was an opportunity for the story of their music and dance to be projected to a nationwide audience. For me, it was a chance to accompany the filming of *Globo Comunidade* and then watch the final product with Ciço when it aired. This meant that I could not only interpret what was included in the edited television program, but also explore why certain moments ended up on the cutting room floor. Even during the filming, the journalist and camera operator made decision after decision, focusing on certain details and downplaying or avoiding others. It turned out that the contrasting depictions of the *samba de coco* families on TV Globo and the members of Cordel in their Brazilian MTV music videos revealed the push and pull of the restorative and reflective nostalgic modes that they were working within. While *samba de coco* was depicted as heritage, with modernity largely erased from the camera's view, the members of Cordel were depicted as individuals living the itinerant life of professional touring musicians, buses, planes, and all. While TV Globo presented the music and dance as part of an unchanging image of the premodern, Cordel performed the migrant who has left home and misses it from afar.

Samba de Coco *as That Which Came Before*

Ciço Gomes and I watched a videotape of the nationally broadcast half-hour television program *Globo Comunidade*. The *samba de coco* dynasties gained access to the national media as part of a seasonal segment celebrating the festival days in June. The program showed the rest of the nation a rural homecoming tradition strongly associated with the Northeast. To celebrate the São João Festival, the program interviewed *samba de coco* musicians in Arcoverde and filmed Coco Raízes and Coco Irmãs Lopes singing and dancing at the *novo cruzeiro*, a large white cross and small chapel perched on a scenic overlook on top of the hills surrounding the city. Coco Raízes is associated in fans' minds with their neighborhood—the old *cruzeiro*—a scenic overlook with a white cement cross on a smaller ledge on the other side of the town. The old *cruzeiro*, built almost a century ago, once offered a view of downtown from its edge. But in the last few decades the city has grown, and houses have sprouted up all around and beyond the old *cruzeiro*. It is now nestled inside the city, alongside the BR-232 highway. The television crew and local tourism officials decided to bring everyone to the *novo cruzeiro* for more dramatic scenery. They began to shoot the opening scene at twilight, with costumed dancers set against the dramatic pinks and deep blues of the quickly darkening sky. Once the sun had set, the camera operator engaged in a graceful ballet with his assistant, who held a powerful light at waist level, staying just out of the camera's range, casting the light of a simulated sunset upon the dancers. Glare from the spotlight blotted out the backdrop of the city behind the partially silhouetted figures.

After sunset Coco Raízes danced down a dirt road to an abandoned rural estate where the scenes depicting the compacting of a mud house's dirt floor would take place. Behind the dancers were the camera operator, his tethered lighting assistant, and the local tourism official who had organized the event, a middle-aged man clad in a tailored black Che Guevara T-shirt. The man behind the camera spent most of the night's procession painfully bent over, his bulky equipment steadied close to the mud for optimum close-ups of the dancers' feet in wooden sandals. Five armed security agents in bulletproof vests hired by the television crew followed at a safe distance off-camera as we walked behind the dancers away from the city lights below.

The television program began with this night scene accompanied by the voice of reporter Karla Almeida referring to *samba de coco* as "history, beauty and tradition" and stating that "to speak of *coco* is to speak of roots [*raízes*]."[2] Leni Lopes was featured explaining that she had been dancing *coco* since she was nine years old. These words were illustrated with a shot of Calixto children dancing on their tile floor in wooden sandals, portraying the unbroken transmission of tradition from generation to generation. As Ciço and I watched the videotape, this juxtaposition was jarring for him. The program erased the protracted feud between the Lopes and Gomes/Calixto families in its telling of the story of *samba de coco* in Arcoverde. Images of social harmony through music and dance prevailed throughout, with interviews conducted in the two competing museums edited together and spliced shots of the feuding groups dancing happily. During one shot the soundtrack featured a song recorded by Coco Raízes that the Lopes sisters claimed was written by their brother Ivo. The song, "Godê Pavão" (Peacock dress), was at the center of the authorship dispute that fueled the conflict between the families.

The night the dancing was filmed, the groups kept strictly to themselves on either side of the uninhabited rural estate. Fagner and Daiane were filmed barefoot, tamping down the mud in front of the house as a demonstration of the dance's origins in joyful communal work. Meanwhile, Coco Irmãs Lopes waited in the school bus, provided by the city, that had brought them up the hill. When the Lopes group finally arrived, its members awaited their turn, staying at least one hundred feet from the filming. I found myself caught in the middle, as I had spent time with both groups but had never been somewhere with both at the same time. I chatted with the Lopes sisters, returned to the filming of Coco Raízes, and then went back to the Lopes side. I was attempting to not demonstrate an allegiance to one group that could be interpreted as a snub by the other. I was not sure that I was succeeding in striking that delicate balance.

A few minutes into the video Severina Lopes explained the story of the dance's social function while sitting in a rocking chair in her front porch museum:

SEVERINA LOPES: Let's take that crude floor and put mud on it. And the owner of the house spread the mud around, he spread it around and flattened it like this. But the mud was still loose, so then, the owner would water it. When it was good and damp, then he would say "Now, Ivo Lopes. The time has come. Let's stomp to tamp the dirt down!" When we started to compact that damp mud . . .
[close-up of her feet in flip-flops demonstrating the step]
. . . and everyone was stomping around, compacting the floor of the house, we did the whole thing together, from one end of the house to the other. And the floor was already getting to be good and ready when everyone arrived there at one end of the house, everyone stepping, then we turned around and did it again, this time to the other corner. Stepping, stepping stepping, the dust settled and the floor got to be well-compacted.
KARLA ALMEIDA: Working and having fun.
SEVERINA LOPES: Working and having fun, because there everyone stepped in a way that was fun.

Almeida's voice-over continued, "It was in the decade of the thirties that residents began to dance *coco* in the city," while slowly panning across the washed-out, sepia-toned photo of Ivo Lopes and his family featured in the Lopes Museum. More juxtapositions of the rival families followed that were jarring for Ciço to watch. Footage of an interview with Iram Calixto

Figure 4.1. Left to right: Assis, Damião, and Iram Calixto being interviewed by TV Globo. *Photo by the author.*

(see figure 4.1), leader of the Gomes/Calixto group Coco Raízes, was included in such a way that her words and her accent emphasized her position outside the Globo network's Rio/São Paulo–dominated mainstream:

IRAM CALIXTO: I plan to make the group grow. There are more Calixtos out there that have been born and that will be born. The only thing is that we want our mission never to end—to keep it going until the end of the world, my world and our world, that is.

KARLA ALMEIDA: Get the word out to other people.

IRAM CALIXTO: Get the word out to other people—and the word has already gone far, you know. Because it's a very beautiful culture, and because it's a very good thing. Very good that—I never thought that we would get all the way to France, and we already have our songs in France, Florianópolis, our music is in Europe.[3] So it's really great. Very marvelous. And culture is a very good thing, very beautiful. And really, I like it a lot. I never thought in my life that Coco Raízes would go as far as it has.

During this segment the tenor of the musicians' responses did not match the voice-over and the images displayed on the screen. Iram's words alternated between pride in *coco* as her culture and pride in her band's success in selling their music. In her answers cultural and commercial sources of pride did not contradict or oppose each other. But as she spoke, I wondered how her words registered with viewers throughout Brazil. Did her accent, grammar, and the grain of her voice engulf the meaning of the words she was saying? Pernambucan accents are distinctive within Brazil, with regional differences in intonation, vocabulary, and idioms. For example, the Calixtos' speech was marked when they pronounced words ending in *te* and *de* as *tee* and *dee*, as opposed to the more ubiquitous pronunciation of *chee* and *gee* heard throughout most of Brazil. In a tightly edited program, Iram's sentence implying that she did not understand that France was in Europe seemed deliberately included to remind the viewer of how remote Arcoverde was and how unsullied by knowledge and the modern world these musicians were. The program as it aired portrayed the group as existing outside modernity and commerce. *Globo Comunidade* completely excised any mention of Coco Raízes's CDs and never shot their audiences or the diverse venues where they regularly perform. There were no shots foregrounding, or even acknowledging, a world powered by electricity and the automobile, other than Ivo's old television and radio displayed mute on a shelf in the Lopes Museum.

Rather than considering herself outside of modernity, Iram is proud to be an enterprising businesswoman. She is pleased with the group's success, and one of her main goals for the group is to play on nationally broadcast variety shows. In fact, Iram allowed me to formally interview her only after I agreed not to ask her about the past. After I convinced her that I wouldn't ask the kinds of questions she didn't want to answer, she was frank about how *samba de coco* represented an avenue for class ascension in a racialized space where, to her, social position was prescribed and immutable: "I was a maid, and Assis was a bricklayer. I was a maid, and today I'm a singer and a producer of a *coco* group. I'm an important person, aren't I? I think that people feel this about us, because they act like they do. Assis was a bricklayer. Today, he is a songwriter. My father worked at the water utility. Today, he plays tambourine and is a singer. Cícero Gomes was a driver. Today, he is a singer. My mother was a housewife. Today she sings backup. My sister is a student. So, some people, not everyone, pass by me and say 'Who are these black people? Today they want to be important.'"

All of these professions are still practiced by the members of Coco Raízes, with the exception of Iram's past work as a maid. But perceptions of them within Arcoverde have changed. Although in 2004 Damião continued to work at the public water utility, he was more often described as Damião do *coco* (of the *coco* group) than as Damião *da compesa* (of the water utility).

Iram's pragmatic, entrepreneurial approach to *samba de coco* is present in the lyrics she has penned as well. The song "Godê Pavão," so vigorously claimed by the Lopes sisters as their family's composition, does contain the following refrain that predates Iram.[4] Whether Iram's late brother Lula, Severina Lopes's brother Ivo, or someone else wrote this refrain remains an open question:

Here comes the old woman from the river's edge
Her dress is "peacock style"

It is "peacock style" and I want to see
The girl cry for a dress like that

Lá vem a velha do ribeirão
O vestido dela é godê pavão

É godê pavão e eu queria ver
A menina chorar pelo godê

After this repeated refrain, however, newer verses written by Iram assert her brother's authorship and define the group's relationship with Cordel in pragmatic marketing terms that sharply contrast the mystical role that Lula Calixto plays within Cordel's mythology:

Cordel Encantado is our good friend
It's culture, it's life (or "it's a living"),
it's promotion

Who wrote this song Godê Pavão
The composition is by Luis Calixto

Cordel Encantado é nosso amigão
É cultura, é vida, é divulgação

Quem fez este coco Godê Pavão
Foi Luis Calixto em composição

The lyrics of Coco Raízes are firmly grounded in the present reality of participating in a tourist economy, and Iram strongly preferred to speak about her current entrepreneurial efforts, not the past. Iram's impatience with the question of *samba de coco*'s origins, however, did not prevent the topic's being of great interest to the journalists who come to Arcoverde to interview musicians. The Globo reporter put it this way in her voice-over during the television program: "A typical dance of the coastal regions of the North and the Northeast, some researchers say that *coco* came to Brazil brought by Africans. The slaves broke open coconuts by hitting the hard outer shells against rocks. From the repetitive sounds emerged the beat. In the middle of all of that noise, the slaves danced a step that mixed the rhythm of their handclaps with that of the coconuts beaten against the rocks and singing."

Accompanying this voice-over, a blurred white square framed the over-exposed images on the screen, marking them off as belonging to another space: a space of memory? the past? a supposed reenactment of slave merriment? The footage, played in slow motion, was not shot in Arcoverde. It was stock footage of a group of elderly people doing a vaguely *coco*-like round dance. Flabbergasted by the stock footage, Ciço could not help but shake his head with a resigned grin. "What is this? Who on earth are they? This isn't *coco*. What is she talking about?"

In the next scene the reporter appeared in the frame, speaking the following into a microphone while Fagner and Daiane danced behind her: "Coco was born in the slave quarters, traveled through the coastal region, and when it arrived in the *sertão*, it transformed. Its verses became poems, its circles filled with samba, and the rhythm became the rhythm of happiness."

The reporter transitioned breathlessly from "slave quarters" to "happiness," revealing an uneasy acknowledgment of the legacy of slavery within a nostalgic narrative regarding the São João holiday. The program presents *samba de coco* in Arcoverde as a puzzling jumble of "befores" to untangle. It was filmed to air all over Brazil on Saint John's Day, a celebration that has become a homecoming tradition for many urban Brazilians—a journey inland from the coast to the interior where rural traditions that have faded in large cities still flicker. This reverse pilgrimage equates the journey inland, from the coast to the desert, with travel back in time. The annual São João Festival anchors this association of the rural and the past in concentric rings as broad as the nation and as local as Arcoverde—or even more rural. Arcoverde is located only three and a half hours from Recife, next to the newly widened BR-232 highway, on the edge of the desert. The city offers the best tourist infrastructure to comfortably host urban pilgrims for a weekend.

Music for the São João Festival season carries with it a bundle of themes and images: dancing by the light of the bonfire; returning to the comforts of a rural home and its traditions. Throughout the television program one sees and hears the performance conflating "that which came before" and "that which happens elsewhere": glimpses of life before electricity and the color photograph; dreams of what it was like before so many people left the arid *sertão* to head for the city. One moment a yesteryear is described in which joyful communal labor blurs the line between work and play, suggesting an egalitarian, utopian space where neighbors stomp the dirt down to finish the floor of a humble, collectively built house. The next moment the dance is declared to have originated in the slave quarters. Another story is told that seems to predate even the slave quarters, hinting at an evolutionary narrative located at the dawn of human history. With its implication of the advent of stone tools, this is not only an origin story for the genre of *coco*, but an origin story for music itself. Instruments as we know them had not yet been invented, but singing, clapping, rocks, and coconuts worked just fine.

Cordel on MTV: "Na Veia" (In My Veins)

The restorative nostalgia of the *Globo Comunidade* program contrasts with the reflective nostalgia rendered in a music video independently produced by Cordel that was shown on Brazilian MTV. TV Globo "purified" and provincialized *samba de coco*, obscuring the contemporary from view. Cordel, in contrast, presented nostalgic longing as the curation of memory of itinerant individuals caught in migratory flows. While comparing the music video with the television program, it is important to keep in mind that the television program was a community outreach show that aired early on a Sunday morning, whereas the music video was produced to be aired on MTV. The local tourism bureau and the Globo television network arranged, shot, and edited the program with no input from the musicians on production decisions. Cordel, in contrast, worked with its producer, exerting significant creative control, and the group's video was shot and edited by Lirinha's then wife, television and film star Leandra Leal.

Cordel's 2005 video for the song "Na veia" (In my veins) begins with a close-up of Lirinha on stage, holding a kerosene lantern next to his face, his eyes closed, the flame almost lapping against his hair. Immediately afterward two wrinkled hands hold several photographs. The hands are gesturing to a photograph of the Alto do Cruzeiro. Over these images Lirinha's voice announces to a spare, guitar-only accompaniment:

> I'm going to sing to *saudade*
> With her red dress
> And her mouth

> I'm going to sing so that *saudade*
> will descend into my head
> and command the party

> *Eu vou cantar pra saudade*
> *Com seu vestido vermelho*
> *E a sua boca*

> *Eu vou cantar pra saudade*
> *Descer na minha cabeça*
> *E comandar sua festa*

A camera shot taken from a moving car scrolls along Arcoverde's pastel-colored row houses, followed by a quick cut to the band members boarding an airplane to the next stop on their tour. Cut to a shot of an elderly woman's hand pointing out her house, a speck in a panoramic newspaper photo celebrating Arcoverde's seventy-fifth anniversary. The camera pans the city below from the vantage point of the Alto do Cruzeiro, and the band members sleep on a bus on their way to their next destination.

Views of the band onstage are interspersed with shots of the musicians holding up mementos to the camera: a Christmas card from 1954, a postcard of an altar at an Afro-Brazilian religious house, Lirinha and his sister Santuza with feathered 1980s hair, a ragged-edged black-and-white photograph of one of Arcoverde's main plazas. The patinas of the photographs jump from decade to decade, from the sepia tone of early twentieth-century photography, to the overexposed outdoor snapshots of the 1970s, to the more precise colors of digital pictures taken just a few years before. The video itself, filmed with a digital camera, has been filtered in postproduction to give it the imperfections and grain of film, complete with the momentary vertical lines and light layer of lint and dust that inevitably settle on a film reel.

Throughout the video the sounds and images are never synchronized. The drum parts shown are not the drum parts heard, nor are the vocal parts shown the vocal parts heard. The video clips of the performances are distanced from the sounds played over the soundtrack, just as the photographs displayed are distanced from the situation in which the images were taken. The effect is that the listener feels the immediacy of the music, but perceives the video images as recollections of past performances, already subject to an inevitable aging process that will consign them to the same fate as faded photographs. Near the end of the video a quick cut reveals Lirinha on stage followed by a four-by-six-inch photograph of this exact scene, only to then return to Lirinha's performance. The song and the video were produced with an awareness that both would soon become memories as well.

> That smell sound image of your body ignites
> and a river full of *saudade* runs through my veins
> In my veins love
> In my veins
> It's like the moonlight that crosses the wall of the jail cell
> It brightens
> More strongly than the sun
>
> *Aquele cheiro som imagem do teu corpo incendeia*
> *E um rio carregado de saudade vem correr na minha veia*

Na veia amor
Na veia
É como a luz da lua que atravessa a parede da cadeia
Clareia
Mais forte que o sol

The images accompanying these lyrics suggest that this rush of emotion is directed toward remembering the families, the hometown, the desert, the past, the girlfriends left behind. By framing the title "In My Veins" in the lyrics as referring to the emotions associated with being at a distance from home, Cordel attempts simultaneously to acknowledge and reject the claim that a place, custom, or style of music is in its blood. While the Globo documentary of *samba de coco* presented a claim to a style firmly rooted in a place and history, Cordel's song foregrounds the constant mediation of photographic images in generating *saudades* and anchoring one to a person or place far away. The video suggests that the song's melancholy is bound up in the hours spent staring out the window that touring musicians experience cooped up on long bus and plane rides. This double movement of the phrase "in my veins" implies that Cordel members are who they are not simply because they are from their hometown, but also because they have moved away from it. By claiming that both being from Arcoverde and longing for Arcoverde from afar are equally embedded in their veins, the group members acknowledge the weight of tradition, while they justify moving their musical style (and their lives) away from the *sertão*.

The video's focus on touring and photographs is just one part of Cordel's deliberate stance against a folkloric aesthetics of staging. Barbara Kirshenblatt-Gimblett summarizes the ascetic approach to performance that they oppose as "a suppression of *representation* markers and a foregrounding of *presentation* markers, an avoidance of the suggestion of 'theater' and an attempt to achieve the quality of pure presence, of a slice of life" (1998, 74). Cordel clearly does not avoid the suggestion of theater in its work. The theme of the CD *O Palhaço do Circo Sem Futuro* (The clown from a good-for-nothing circus without a future) (2002) also confirms that theatricality and spectacle are central to the group's shows.

In the song "In My Veins," *saudade* is described as a spirit that possesses bodies like an Afro-Brazilian deity, personified as a seductress in a red dress, and portrayed as an addictive drug. In the last verse, as the percussion grows more intense, Lirinha adds to these comparisons, roaring:

When *saudade* arrives
With its battalions of agitators and so many flags
I will sing

Quando a saudade chegar
Com seu batalhão de agitadores e tanta bandeira
Vou cantar

Describing *saudade* as a political demonstration could simply be a way to describe intensity of emotion. However, considering Lirinha's stated desire to create a "spectacle that also has this thing of release, of a history of much repression . . . wanting to explode the repression of the Northeast," it is conceivable to read the lyric as depicting *saudade* as a political agenda that he's singing against—state-sponsored nostalgia like that in the *Globo Comunidade* program. Despite this stated goal, however, an unexpected thing happened. As Cordel toured Brazil and paid tribute to its hometown at every show, it inspired its fans to go visit Arcoverde, fueling the tourism industry that sustained the kind of nostalgia the group sang against.

The music video's opening shot of hands holding a photo of the Alto do Cruzeiro is book-ended near the end of the video with a view of the cement cross taken from inside a car as it approaches the overlook. A small cross on a rosary dangles from the rearview mirror. The Alto do Cruzeiro is empty. The music ends with another panoramic view of Arcoverde taken from the Alto do Cruzeiro. After the music has ended, a collage of the band members' voices, close-miked and intimate, lists the people and places that give them *saudades*. The clip ends with Lirinha filming his young daughter, who lives in Arcoverde and sees him mainly when he visits, playing in a kid-sized, circus-themed play tent.

The empty Alto do Cruzeiro overlook in the video's closing image stands in stark contrast to the *samba de coco* documentary, with its many picturesque scenes shot near a cross overlooking town. It also provides a counterpoint to Cordel's other music video, filmed for the song "Chover (ou invocação para um dia líquido)" (Rain [or invocation for a liquid day]), recorded before Cordel moved away from the Northeast to São Paulo. Halfway through "Chover," when Lirinha and Clayton bellow that "rain has fallen!," the scene cuts abruptly from the band playing alone in rocky, parched, moonscape-like rural terrain to the Alto do Cruzeiro midcelebration, teeming with *samba de coco* musicians and their fans.

Lula Calixto not only influenced the band's music, but also entered the group's lyrics as a figure embodying folk celebration. Of the many climaxes of this song, the greatest release comes right after the declaration that the rain has indeed fallen. At this moment the first image described is that of "Lula Calixto Becoming Mateus" (*Lula Calixto virando Mateus*). At the apex of the song's dramatic arc, Lula Calixto is invoked to indicate that with the rain comes the celebration. He is described as in the process of shedding his everyday identity and putting on the pointy hat and shiny clothes that indicate his transformation into the protean figure Mateus, the jester of the *reisado*.

"Drinking from the wellspring" (*bebendo da fonte*), a phrase used by Recife musicians who turn to poorer, often older musicians for inspiration, is enacted, and this contact is as reinvigorating as a drought-ending downpour. As the music features the accented steps of dancing *coco* in wooden sandals, the musicians from Cordel dance with their friends in Coco Raízes. The camera weaves between the members of Cordel and Coco Raízes stomping the exaggerated steps of an aggressive, camera-friendly *coco* that matches the heavier sound of Cordel's layers of percussion.

In the final shots of the "Chover" video, the profile of Damião Calixto, one of the patriarchs of Coco Raízes, is shown as he smiles and sings along. Cut to a retreating aerial shot revealing the whole group playing amid the crowd, no stage or division separating the two. Return to the ground, where Lirinha gestures toward Assis Calixto, the other living Coco Raízes patriarch, who is playing the shaker. Lirinha puts his arm around Assis's shoulder. The final shot of the video frames the entire Alto do Cruzeiro overlook. At the foot of the cross, which is festooned with lightbulbs, burns a bonfire, and behind the overlook the city lights speckle the night sky. The band stands in a small circle cleared out among the assembled bystanders. The crowd applauds heartily.

Performing the Migrant, Performing Home

Frontier territories and social fractures, mythical lands laden with symbolism and signs, the *sertão* (arid backlands) and the *favelas* (slums) have always been the "other side" of modern and positivist Brazil. They are places of misery, mysticism and the disinherited, non-places and paradoxically places of picture postcard beauty, with their storehouses of "typicality," where tradition and invention are extracted from adversity.

Ivana Bentes (Nagib 2003, 121)

While *samba de coco* performs the premodern origins of the Brazilian nation, the members of Cordel, in their "In My Veins" video, perform their contemporary, itinerant life as touring musicians—buses, planes, electricity, and all. The essence of their identity (what is "in their veins") is argued to be nostalgia produced by dislocation; they claim their emotional reaction to flux as what is unchangeable about them. This move acknowledges flux and dislocation from the outset, revising essentialist, nativist claims. In their first video, "Chover," the focus was on finding inspiration in the traditions of poor and often old musicians anointed as culture bearers. By sharing a celebration in the Alto do Cruzeiro with *samba de coco* musicians, they asserted their proximity to *sertão* tradition to be a source of their distinctiveness unavailable to those in the coastal capital. The later "In My Veins" video, however, refuses to re-create the drama of solidarity performed in the "Chover" video, instead representing the band's new circumstances living in São Paulo. It foregrounds photographs and mementos instead, as tokens that invoke group members' individual, reflective nostalgia.

The *Globo Comunidade* program on *samba de coco*, in contrast, erases the trappings of modernity to create a romanticized space projecting a jumble of "befores." The *samba de coco* groups, as framed by the local tourism bureau and the Globo network, are being inserted into the idealized register of the "past taken as essence, as national mythical origin, as an experience of the lost union between human beings and nature" (Xavier 1997, 14).

In the shifting contemporary national imaginary, *samba de coco* and Cordel do Fogo Encantado have proven uneasily dependent on each other. While *samba de coco* performs a multicultural twist on an older narrative of national mythical origins, Cordel has grappled with and ultimately attempted to refuse the role it has inherited from Mário de Andrade and others of "drinking from the wellspring": drawing inspiration from and updating tradition.

This refusal was derived from the group's growing discomfort with the concepts of tradition and *cultura popular* (folk or traditional culture), which Lirinha believes are fragile: "Let's say that Cordel do Fogo Encantado isn't *popular*. Lia de Itamaracá is *cultura popular*. Or, then, Mestre Salustiano is *popular*, Cordel isn't. Why is Mestre Salustiano *popular* and Cordel isn't? It isn't CD sales. So, I start to think that the measure is poverty. *Popular* is linked to poverty, to incorrect Portuguese. From there come definitions that are even crazier still, like *popular* is when you inherit an oral tradition from your family and repeat it, without understanding it, without processing it. I still don't understand the definition of *cultura popular*. It's fragile to me, even though it is in all the books that I read. I don't get it, what is popular and regional poetry."

The idea Lirinha decried as "crazier still"—that *cultura popular* is a matter of inheriting and repeating a family tradition with little creative transformation to its form and content—remained at the core of the *Globo Comunidade* representation of the *samba de coco* families. Lirinha's critique reflects shifts in the band's thinking on cultural rescue in the wake of their early success and increasing unease with being associated with the informal salvage ethnography that they dramatize in their earlier music video.

At the beginning of their careers, Cordel treated Coco Raízes in a mythical register that rather resembled the *Globo Comunidade* depiction, despite Cordel's best efforts to complicate this dynamic between "innovator" and "source" later on.

While *samba de coco* performs national origins for visitors from the coast and viewers all over Brazil, the featured musicians consider their work to be firmly grounded in the present. When Iram Calixto speaks forcefully of her class ascension and business goals for the group, and when Ciço looks at the TV screen and says, "What is this? This isn't *coco*," they are questioning the spatial and temporal distancing embedded in the TV Globo documentary. The group is striving to be seen as part of the national "here and now." When members of Coco Raízes speak about the power that they feel when they are on stage in front of hundreds of people, they express how exhilarating it is to be so visible within Pernambuco. But they are aware that this visibility involves trade-offs.

Marilyn Ivy's work (1995) on Japanese modernity and tradition speaks to the "uncanny instability" of *samba de coco* in Arcoverde's performance of home. She sees nostalgic appeals to premodernity, like those depicted by *Globo Comunidade*, as attempts to reassure in a context of unease about the stability of cultural transmission. The related fear of cultural grey-out in the face of globalization also contributes to the popularity of *samba de coco*. Cordel uses the marginal-turned-traditional sounds of *samba de coco* to shore up its stance in relation to these concerns—holding *samba de coco* as a vanishing tradition that should be valued and portraying the group members as modern Brazilians who haven't forgotten their past. In this process *samba de coco* is framed as a representative cultural survival holding back the loss of the past. This role, thrust upon *samba de coco* musicians, has complicated their dreams of "making it" as professional musicians. When I met the then managers of Coco Raízes in 2004, they confided that they advised the group not to travel too much, for fear that band members would lose their cultural identities. Assis Calixto, the main songwriter of the group, countered: "I've lived here a long time. My bags are packed. I'd love to travel to the South," just as Cordel did. The stage manager at the time wanted to experiment with the staging of the group's show, but he was aware of the risk of *fugindo da proposta* or "getting off track" and being considered merely a commercial pop band. Group members are aware that appearing ambitious could cost them their status as representative cultural survivals, which could cost them their audience and cause them to forfeit their role in the local tourist economy. The tourist economy, in turn, helps reproduce the arid northeastern interior as a nostalgic space of *saudade*.

A Favela Light *in the* Sertão Light: *Afro-Pernambucan Tourism and the Cosmetics of Hunger*

Middle- and upper-class Brazilians going up a hill to visit a *favela* to "drink from the source" is a practice embedded in the lore of Brazilian popular music at least since Noel Rosa's success helped nationalize and popularize the practice in the 1920s and 1930s (Vianna and Chasteen 1999, 87). A scene in the film *Rio Zona Norte* (1957) dramatizes the practice of slumming in the hilltop shantytowns of Rio de Janeiro. Arcoverde's recent cultural tourism boom combines a rural sojourn associated with the saint's days in June with an urban trek up the hill to dance in a poorer neighborhood.

Several factors converged in the late 1990s, above and beyond the distinctive and powerful voices of Coco Raízes and Cordel, to create a shift in the town's visibility. One broad national trend regarding race and national identity in the postdictatorship 1990s was the persistent questioning of the consensus that social celebrations such as samba musically reproduce and represent the harmonious integration of races and social classes in Brazil. Assertions of black cultural difference stemmed from the black movement's questioning of the rhetoric of racial democracy and celebration of racial and cultural mixture. The popularity of hip-hop and funk among *favela* youths is seen by Yúdice as one such indicator of this "disarticulation of national identity" (2003, 114).

In addition, since the 1980s in the northeastern city of Salvador, Bahia, musical expressions of Afro-Brazilian identity have quickly proved highly lucrative for cultural tourism by both domestic and foreign visitors. Coco Raízes's alliances with coastal *coco* and *afoxé* groups and the participation of Damião Calixto and some of his immediate family in a local *umbanda terreiro* point to the group's links with the Afro-Brazilian religious and activist communities. In this neoliberal multiculturalist context, Arcoverde's municipal government had different reasons to emphasize Afro-Brazilian cultural manifestations in the interior *sertão*. For the tourism bureau, placing *samba de coco* on the town's campaigns of self-promotion was a way to differentiate their São João celebration from those of larger nearby cities such as Caruaru and Campina Grande, who market the event with the rural kitsch of white and *mestiço* hick clowns dancing to *forró* and *quadrilha*. Arcoverde attracted a younger, more fashionable musical visitor from Recife who enjoyed the Afro-Pernambucan elements in Recife's Carnaval and the rooted cosmopolitanism of the state capital's post–*mangue beat* new music scene. Arcoverde has been called *sertão light*, because of its relatively amenable climate, nestled in a small valley on the edge of the desert. A journey away from the urban tension of Recife to the Alto do Cruzeiro can be seen as a visit to *favela light*[5] in the *sertão light*, where one can "drink from the source" safely and comfortably, enjoying warm, small-town hospitality and spontaneous musical performances. If times have changed, and the semblance of harmony between races and classes is increasingly difficult to sustain in the urban space, this movement to the hinterlands can be seen as a nostalgic retreat to the fading dream that "everything sooner or later ends up in samba" (Yúdice 2003, 112).

PART II

CHAPTER FIVE

Festival

During the first week of June 2004 a temporary *casa de taipa*, a house made out of mud, was erected in downtown Arcoverde's main traffic circle (see figure 5.1). During the ten days of the São João Festival, it would serve as a museum in honor of two *samba de coco* musicians: Lula Calixto and Ivo Lopes. Once completed, the mud shack resembled those found on the outskirts of town and in nearby rural areas. Within the festival area, the mud house was located in the center of a staged village portraying the first settlement of Arcoverde. As workers slapped mud on a frame of wooden slats, poor Arcoverdenses inquired about the prospect that the government was building free housing for the poor on such prime real estate. They asked if they could be placed on a waiting list. After the previous year's festival, a family had squatted in a mud house in the traffic circle until the municipal government, fearing political fallout from the episode, paid for their bus tickets to leave town.

The confusion between the intended purpose of the mud house as a temporary museum and the perception that it was a coveted dwelling condenses a tension underlying the festival. The mud house museum plays a role in a narrative of civic progress implied in the spatial layout of the São João Festival. The staged village anchors the festival's epicenter to the city's past, conjuring a caricatured image of the town's origins. This example of "what came before," constructed of mud and palm leaves, serves as a contrast to zones framed as modern and contemporary. By placing a mud house in the center of town and presenting it as an artifact from the past, the city is doing more than merely creating a quaint festival atmosphere; the mud hut can also be seen as a reminder of how far the city has come in its seven decades of existence. The appearance of squatters and waiting list seekers, however, disrupts this attempt to banish mud houses to the past, serving as a reminder that similar shelter persists today on the poorest edges of town.

By 2004 several competing narratives could be discerned within the São

Figure 5.1. The mud hut museum in the staged village in the center of town. *Photo by Paulo Britto. Courtesy of the Journal Portal do Sertão.*

João Festival. The municipal government attempted to place a range of performances within an overarching teleological narrative representing certain groups as Arcoverde's past and others as its present and future. These efforts were evident in the spatial configuration and decorations of various festival zones, each with a contrasting performance venue. The delineation of these zones—from a nostalgic "staged village" reenacting the town's origins to a contemporary stage with a conspicuous display of state-of-the-art technology—betrayed the administration's mixed feelings toward the marginal-turned-traditional musicians placed on display to prove that the city remembers its cultural roots. What at first glance appeared to be simply a celebration of a place and all of its inhabitants, upon further scrutiny reveals an ascending series of stages, in both senses of the word: stages of development and scaffolded stages upon which musicians perform.

The spatial organization of the festival revealed a tension between the state-sponsored festival's rhetoric of social inclusion and the persistence of severe social inequality that undercuts the full cultural citizenship of a large portion of the population. Richard Flores's analysis of the "re-membering" and "dis-membering" of a social body through the performance of Los Pastores in San Antonio, Texas, resonates here. Like the Los Pastores troupe, performers in Arcoverde struggle—with varying success—against the performers and the audience becoming "dis-membered from the present" and each other (Flores and Benmayor 1997, 146) by the processes that package a cultural form for touristic consumption.

Cordel, and subsequently Coco Raízes, have leveraged their success in Recife and throughout Brazil to raise their stature locally within the festival. By 2004 they were not just performing on the smaller, rustic, cultural/traditional stage as they had in years past, but also headlining on the main stage—now named after Lula—at the festival's most important moment on Saint John's Day. But despite this hard-won recognition, both groups continued to struggle against being viewed through a blurred lens of national-cultural nostalgia as fetishes of culture loss, ultimately distanced from the national "here and now."

Music and Politics in Arcoverde

During the year I lived in Arcoverde, politics and music were closely entangled. Music enlivened political events and helped delineate constituencies; politics shaped the city's soundscape by structuring events and valorizing or ignoring genres. City-sponsored concerts echoed at high volume from the plaza, audible in an expansive concentric ring around downtown, reaching half of the city until early in the morning. Announcers declared the concerts to be a service the current administration was offering, placing the cultural events on a par with infrastructural projects and other government initiatives.

During the campaign season trucks flanked with large speakers delivered tape loops of relentless political jingles as they drove through the town's residential neighborhoods. There were several *showmícios*, a newly coined term combining entertainment—a show—with a *comício* or political meeting. Two main types of *showmícios* took place during the campaign: a stationary *showmício* and an *arrastão*. At a stationary *showmício*, one side of the temporary stage was crammed with the candidate's family and political allies. A band—usually a *forró estilizado* group—played on the other side of the stage.[1] The candidates then clapped and swayed, to give the impression that they liked the music. The fact that the candidates were willing to dance to the same music as the cheering crowd was used as a display of solidarity with the voters in the audience. The singers, for their part, added rhymes praising the candidates and led cheers between the songs.

During the São João Festival the nexus of music and politics was not as obvious as it is at the campaign *showmícios*. There were no cheers for candidates during the festival. Nevertheless, in subtle and not-so-subtle ways, the municipal government's efforts to frame the meaning of the festival permeated its structure and how Arcoverdenses understood it. It was not uncommon for performers to recognize politicians and other important figures in the audience, thanking them for their presence or exclaiming, for example, "[The mayor] Doutora Rosa sure likes to dance *samba de coco!*" São João played a part in what I heard many call the *pastoril político*, meaning that the colors one wore to the festival connoted one's allegiance to a political party and its candidates.[2] Candidates bought matching T-shirts for traditional groups in their party's colors. An internal struggle took place within one traditional group over the colors of members' matching outfits.

São João Begins: The Downtown Festival Area

On the principal downtown traffic circle, music categorized as "traditional" and "cultural" was played in a *palhoça*, a temporary, wall-less shelter with a stage decorated with palm fronds. The principal attractions on the Ivo Lopes stage, night after night, were *samba de coco*, *reisado*, and other folkloric groups. This performance venue festooned with markers of rusticity was located next to a staged village advertised as reenacting the town's origins (see figure 5.2).

In the center of the staged village stood a thatched-roof gazebo. Under its canopy one or two couples danced *forró*, dressed in exaggerated, clownlike representations of *matutos* (rural hicks). The band members stood in a closed circle on the pavement next to the thatched gazebo, dressed in the colors of Rosa Barros's political coalition—matching yellow shirts and red handkerchiefs around their necks—stone-faced as they played for hours at a time.

As I proceeded farther west, past the gazebo, the traditional/cultural area in the center of the festival quickly gave way to a gauntlet of makeshift bars leading to the large open area where the audience stood, their backs to the staged village, and listened to the events at the Lula Calixto main stage. The area outside the staged village was thoroughly plastered with beer ads featuring a nationally prominent spokesmodel dressed as a *matuta*. To the right were two stories of *camarotes*, temporarily erected VIP party rooms where people in politics, business, and the press pay for a privileged vantage point of the scene.

SAMBA DE COCO RAÍZES DE ARCOVERDE

Coco Raízes was the most visible group in São João promotional materials. Tourism magazines and pamphlets carried images of the group. After years of playing a minor role in the annual festival, Coco Raízes's success at Recife's Carnaval and elsewhere raised their stature at home. The main stage

Figure 5.2. Gigantic wooden sandals and rag doll *samba de coco* dancers welcome festivalgoers. *Photo by Paulo Britto. Courtesy of the Journal Portal do Sertão.*

of the festival was named in honor of Lula Calixto, and Coco Raízes were the only group performing at São João that performed on both the cultural stage and the main stage (see figure 5.3).

The two families were experts at engineering a jubilant mood, succeeding in coaxing even the most hesitant audience to dance. Ciço Gomes and his son Fagner constantly sought eye contact with the audience. Much of the appeal of the group derived from their virtuoso feet, hands, and tongues. Vocal skills came in the form of improvisation and rapid-fire dexterity. Ciço Gomes was the only singer in the group who improvised verses, but many others sang impressively quickly. Under layers of interlocking percussion parts, the dancers performed hard-stepping patterns wearing the kind of wooden sandals featured in the festival area's archway. A section of the stage floor was covered with a piece of plywood to amplify the dance, and a microphone captured the rumbling railroad-like sounds, adding them to the PA system's mix. During their seven festival performances, the dancers were perpetually running back and forth between the stage and the street to coax audience members to dance.

Coco Raízes's performances centered around the themes of tradition and family. The lead singer Ciço Gomes introduced each member of the three generations of Calixtos and Gomeses, detailing their family relationships. He made sure the crowd knew that their matching clothes were hand-sewn

Figure 5.3. Coco Raízes performing on the main stage. Photo by Paulo Britto.
Courtesy of the Journal Portal do Sertão.

by his wife, Dona Maria. The group projected an image of humble families—unified, extended, functional—who celebrated together in musical and social harmony.

<h3 style="text-align:center">REISADO DAS CARAÍBAS</h3>

When the Reisado das Caraíbas began to perform at the Ivo Lopes cultural stage, the music sounded terrific from afar—the PA system was crystal clear. As I approached, however, it was difficult to see the performers, obscured by the crowd. I squeezed into a decent vantage point and saw that the elderly musicians were nowhere to be found. Suddenly I realized that the music consisted of selections from Carlos Sandroni's recent field recording session, which I had attended a few months before (*Responde a roda outra vez* 2005). The recording, which was made as part of a preservationist effort supporting the *reisado* group, had given the children's dance troupe the independence to perform without the adults. Later that night I talked to Sandra, who spearheaded the children's *reisado* while working for the state sponsoring culture. Despondent, she told me that the majority of the adults in the *reisado* allied themselves with the opposition candidate and had decided for that reason that they could not perform at this year's São João Festival.

The children were tugged along by the unforgiving tempo of the CD.

Without the eye contact of the Mestre, or some kind of warning before beginning the song, the dancers took a couple of measures to find the beat after the next CD track unexpectedly began. In between songs there was little time for applause. A television news camera focused a blindingly bright light on their reflective costumes. In my camcorder recording of the television crew's filming of the event, the dancer closest to their camera dissolved into a glowing ball of light. The dancers' movements were regimented, and their faces remained serious as they executed stomping scissor steps to a simple, heavy 3/4 beat.

CORDEL DO FOGO ENCANTADO

Cordel do Fogo Encantado performed its annual homecoming show on the main stage. From my vantage point, not far from the police turret manned by an officer surveying the crowd, I could see across the plaza to the VIP party rooms. A sample of melismatic *aboio* cattle-herding song floated from the left stack of speakers to the right and back again. The band emerged from the fog and colored lights that filled the stage. Three percussionists played layers of bass drums, congas, tom-toms, and cymbals in a thunderous percussion groove. Lirinha launched into a frenzied dance that resembled a marionette desperately trying to break free from the strings that controlled it. Portraying his life as an itinerant musician who missed home, he continued to yell/sing, declaring that he would marry his *saudades*, and that this feeling of loss would become his intimate companion. At one point midsong, he exclaimed, "My dear city!" (see figure 5.4).

Throughout the performance Lirinha used gestures and props to contribute to a given song's dramatic impact (see figure 5.5). As he sang about vengeful justice coming to a *favela*, bullet sound effects caused him to convulse as if riddled with automatic gunfire. Fog, colored lights, and strobe lights accompanied songs about rain and storms, and spinning, flashing lights emulated an approaching police car. As he intoned over relentless percussion, red lights shone laser stigmata emanating from his palms. As he recited a poem, he illuminated his face with a kerosene lantern. While smearing sinister clown makeup onto his face, he screamed that he was a clown in a circus without a future.[3]

Near the show's end the members of the band played a medley of a song they had learned from Lula Calixto and a chorus that Reisado das Caraíbas would use to open their performances. The song title "Foguete de reis (ou a guerra)" was derived from the interchangeable local use of the words *foguete* (firecracker) and *folguedo* (celebration), when referring to fast, raucous marches (foguetes de roda) in the *samba de coco* repertoire. Cordel's use of this

Figure 5.4. Cordel do Fogo Encantado performing on the main stage. *Photo by Paulo Britto. Courtesy of the Journal Portal do Sertão.*

conflation brought together associations of mass celebration and mass violence, and the song ended with the sound effect of a roman candle exploding.

At the festival a busload of members of the Cordel fan club had arrived from Recife earlier that day. The audience was divided between diehard fans screaming, moshing, and singing along in the area in front of the stage and the people in the two elevated areas on either side. Facing the stage, to the left were the VIP galleries, where local professionals mingled with fairly disinterested, neutral expressions. On the other side were small outdoor bars that charged a fee to reserve groups of tables. This reservation system meant that most of the people sitting at these tables were middle- and upper-class families from Arcoverde. During the performance much of this section of the crowd appeared positively stunned. Others looked curious and baffled, as if trying to fathom how such an unfamiliar treatment of familiar cultural elements had become synonymous with their city elsewhere in Brazil. For these Arcoverdenses, Cordel's staged Arcoverde did not resemble the lived Arcoverde.

The bulk of acts playing on the main stage were elaborately staged *forró estilizado* groups. Cordel's brooding style starkly contrasted with the relentlessly upbeat mood of most of the other groups sharing this stage for the festival's ten nights. Watching the range of audience members' expressions reminded me of speaking earlier with a clerk at one of the local hotels that

Figure 5.5. An anguished Lirinha in front of the backdrop for the Clown in the Circus without a Future tour. *Photo by Paulo Britto. Courtesy of the Journal Portal do Sertão.*

hosted Cordel's fans from Recife. When I asked him what performances he was going to attend at the festival, he responded, *forró estilizado*. He liked close *forró* dancing with his girlfriend and insisted that *forró estilizado* was much closer to the local reality. Cordel's fans, in contrast, he insisted, were out of touch with reality. From behind the counter in the hotel lobby, he mused that Cordel's fans had probably never even worked a day in their lives, hinting at a class divide between the band's fan base and the bulk of the festival.

Before ending their set, Cordel endorsed Cobaias (Guinea Pigs), commanding rock fans to go immediately across the street to the circus tent where the band was waiting to play.

COBAIAS (GUINEA PIGS)

On the other side of the main thoroughfare, outside the cordoned-off festival area was a line of booths proffering foosball, shooting galleries, and concessions. Next to a meager assortment of rickety amusement park rides stood a circus tent. Rock bands with names such as Cobaias (Guinea Pigs) and Crucificados pelo Sistema (Crucified by the System) played under the big top. I was setting up my equipment to record Cobaias when a teenager approached me to confirm that tonight was the night Pastor was going to sing. His palpable excitement foreshadowed the reverence with which Cobaias' congregation of young fans regarded the band's appropriately named lead singer, Pastor. With long dreadlocks and a worn Che Guevara T-shirt, Pastor led his flock as they moshed in a circular pattern around the center tent pole.

From the moment that the group was introduced, a musical line in the sand was drawn. A friend of the band members stepped up to the mic and roundly criticized *forró estilizado*, música sertaneja, vacuous pop—much of the music played down the street at the main stage. The MC incited the crowd, who jeered at these bands whose fan base, he believed, consisted of people who accepted what television foisted upon them. The tent was situated only a block or two away from the central area of the festival, but because of its placement across a relatively busy thoroughfare, it was isolated from the rest of São João, spatially as well as in terms of collective mood. The band played heavy rock/punk grooves while Pastor growled lyrics full of righteous indignation about social inequality, hypocrisy, poverty, and restrictive social roles. In stark contrast to the perpetual celebration within the main festival area, under the circus tent there was a perception that Pastor was singing truth to power, and his followers were listening reverently as they churned around the tent pole.

Introducing the song "Fevereiro," Pastor clarified: "We have never been and will never be against Carnaval. We are against the media that uses popular festivals to cover up the inequality and social ills of this rotten society." After decrying the murder of street children, rape, political corruption, and drug violence over a muscular guitar riff, the entire band added bitter outrage to the chorus that hinges on diversion as both "fun" and "distraction":

> But in February
> All of this is forgotten
> It's time to play
> It's the month with the most diversion
>
> . . .
>
> This is the country of Carnaval
> This is the Carnaval of Brazil
> For eleven months the country goes badly
> February is the greatest
>
> Fucking hell
>
> *Mas eis que em fevereiro*
> *Tudo isso é esquecido*
> *É hora de brincar*
> *É o mês mais divertido*
>
> . . .
>
> *Esse é o país do Carnaval*
> *Assim é o Carnaval do Brasil*
> *Por onze meses o país vai mal*
> *Fevereiro é a nota mil*
> *Puta que pariu*

Despite the song's references to carnaval, not São João, it was clear to the audience that its critique of the state's perceived ability to use music as a distraction resonated with the current setting. Strengthening this bridge between urban poverty and Arcoverde, Pastor ended "Fevereiro" by reciting bleak lines from Chico Buarque's "Construção" (*Construction*), which suggests that the oppressive social order during the years of the military dictatorship was more fragile than it seemed.[4] It recounts the story of a construction worker's last day. The protagonist's social invisibility as a member of the working poor means that his fatal fall from the scaffolding does not provoke compassion from passersby. Instead, drivers only care that the incident caused a traffic jam on their day off:

He died on the wrong side of the street, disrupting traffic

Morreu na contramão, atrapalhando tráfego

The threat of violence at the event, however, caused this social criticism to be trumped by the perceived need for physical security. In 2004 the administration had sponsored the rock stage for the first time since it had been shut down four years before after bands used the PA system to scream obscenities at politicians. The performers were acutely aware of how tenuous this support was. Despite their diatribes lobbed at easy targets like cheesy pop stars, they graciously thanked the mayor's office for its support. They were also outspoken in thanking the security guards for being there for everyone's safety, both before the event and later, when someone threatened to use a knife in the mosh pit. Pastor preached peace and praised the police for subduing the knife-wielding teen. It was a delicate situation for a band with such strident antiestablishment rhetoric.

The Alto do Cruzeiro Tourist Destination

The Alto do Cruzeiro was far enough from the center of town that only fans of Coco Raízes would make the trek. A thatch-roofed structure blocked off the cobblestone street lined with rows of small houses.

Lula's brother Assis, the main songwriter of Coco Raízes, invited me into his small house. The main room measured approximately six by ten feet. Between the television stand and the couch there was only room for one person to stand comfortably. Two slender, tan urbanites in their twenties tentatively came to the doorway. Assis invited them in. They were excited, wide-eyed, and uncomfortable, looking around the small house. The moment betrayed the ambiguity of Assis's social status; recognition of Assis as an artist partially inverted traditional class hierarchies, but had not translated into a significant financial windfall for him. The scene could be seen as an encounter between a revered artist and his doting fans, between poorer people and richer people, between darker-skinned people and lighter-skinned people, or all of the above.

The urban fans' reverence for Assis was predicated on their perception of *samba de coco* as the embodiment of premodern cultural memory. The preservation of the genre, however, was facilitated by a rural past located not before or outside modernity, but on its margins, subject to its dangers while excluded from its benefits. Assis and Lula grew up in a thatched-roof mud house in the arid *sertão* outside of Arcoverde, coming to the city fifty years before when their father found work erecting telephone poles for the electric company. Practices such as *samba de coco*, ignored or disdained by the middle classes less than a generation before, were now celebrated for their refusal to succumb to mass-mediated consumer culture.

I ventured into the Calixtos' bar. Unexpectedly, I recognized two acquaintances from Recife, Daniel and Camila, and sat down to talk to them at a table with several of their friends. I asked Daniel why he thought that people came to Arcoverde from Recife for São João, and he responded that the "culture of high-rise apartment buildings" in Recife was cutting off cultural ties between people. As a result, in his view, there simply was not the same kind of strong cultural solidarity there that one can find in a place that still has traditional culture like Arcoverde.

He explained that Arcoverde was becoming the destination for those who were turned off by how stylized they believed the São João festivities had become in nearby interior cities such as Caruaru. According to Daniel, there was a demographic of people who found Caruaru's enormous marketplace of handicrafts, *quadrilha* line-dance contests, and quaint *bandas de pífano* an inauthentic tourist trap. He believed Arcoverde was capitalizing on this impression by offering a São João festival more weighted toward *samba de coco*, *reisado*, and other traditional music.

A drunk friend of Daniel's insisted that many of the visitors considered themselves superior to those from the small city. He interjected bluntly, "Yeah, well, people from Recife think they're better than people from, for example, Caruaru." Daniel added diplomatically that they had been talking earlier about rivalries between cities in the area. His friend refused to soften his statement: "No. You can just see it on their faces." He gestured to the tall, well-fed, cosmopolitan crowd isolated from the festival's center: "There's just something in their expressions. A lot of the people here think they're better than people from smaller towns."

At the Alto do Cruzeiro, Assis played multiple roles as performer, host, and souvenir salesman. The younger women in the Calixto family—Iram,

Iuma, Daiane, and Damaris—also shifted between stations when they weren't performing: tending bar, waiting tables, dancing with visitors, networking, and generally making sure that everyone was in high spirits. They were the stars, the hosts, and the service staff. The smaller children also entertained the crowd, wowing them with their precocious facility at dancing and playing instruments. It was common for an older member of the family to call over three-year-old Luizinho and ask him to show off his dance steps, sing a song, or play a drum. At one performance Assis and his grandnephew sang a duet in which they sang in harmony, "It was a small house, but it was full of love." Almost without fail, this led audience members to comment on how impressive his musical abilities were for his age and to gush about how wonderful it was that they were passing on their traditional knowledge so early, to safeguard the unbroken continuation of the *samba de coco* tradition in Arcoverde.

Stages of Development at the São João Festival

The festival's story of civic progress follows a path from the thatched gazebo to the large, fully equipped principal stage, with its imposing stacks of enormous speakers. Not far from the main stage named in Lula Calixto's honor stood the mud house museum that squatters envied. It unwittingly resembled the kind of shack known to aid the transmission of Chagas disease, the disease of poverty that had taken Lula's life five years before. The thatch harbors an insect that serves as the Chagas disease vector. The official script suggested by the juxtaposition of the gazebo/mud houses and the main stage's impressive show of technology leaves little room for the messy contradictions of this symbolic gesture of social inclusion. One may surmise, for example, that better public hospital care for Arcoverde's poor may have kept Lula Calixto alive. Instead, he was made posthumously into a hero of popular culture, and his portrait was hung in the quaint mud house museum at the symbolic center of the festival. The narrative implicitly told to festivalgoers walking through mud house lane to the modern stage is a teleological narrative of modernization—the story of the city's progress. The stages erected for musical performances are framed as stages of development.

The slippage between the rural, the primitive, the traditional, and the local hints that this story is being told on many nesting levels. São João, to residents of larger Brazilian cities, has become a time of year to travel to the *sertão* and get in touch with the nation's rural roots. To many from the South, the entire Northeast suffices as a space of nostalgia. For some Recifenses, Caruaru is becoming too industrialized in its assembly line approach to celebrating tradition; Arcoverde wins their tourist dollar with a more rustic, more "authentic" product, considered a more effective counterbalance to the alienation of "high-rise apartment building culture." Within Arcoverde proper the poor are incorporated into a developmentalist vision of the city through the use of traditional musicians for emblematic purposes. The result is an ambivalent mixture of celebration and scorn, homage and appropriation of the marginal turned representative.

Cordel's turbulent artistic vision adopts heavy metal's aura of danger in an attempt to avoid being labeled folklore or celebratory regionalism. Although the group attempts a theatrical exorcism of the sedimented stereotypes of the northeastern *sertão* region, the question remains whether the use of traditional styles helps Cordel accomplish this goal. The festival performances detailed above suggest that its constant tributes to *reisado* and *samba de coco* traditions result in further distancing these traditional groups from the local here and now at the same time that they contribute to opening up performance opportunities for the professionalizing traditional musicians. Cordel's popularity arose at a moment when the promotion of cultural tourism reached deeper into the interior of the state, leading to a complex interplay of social exclusion and inclusion emblematic of Brazil's disjunctive democracy. These musicians actively participate, with varying degrees of success, in a cultural politics of recognition. At the same time, they also participate in performances that partially erase their modernity, distance them from the contemporary, and through caricature, threaten to foreclose their cultural citizenship.

Consider, for example, Reisado das Caraíbas. The musicians in the group did not show up for their show, despite the fact that they were prominently displayed, second only to Coco Raízes, in the festival's promotional literature as an example of the region's cultural riches. Their political opposition to the event notwithstanding, previous stage performances had left them frustrated, contributing to their hesitation. Most of the members are elderly, and at the time they were in a painful moment in their efforts to stage a performance that was traditionally performed roaming from home to home. This became clear at events where their performances were truncated from three hours to ten minutes. Their discomfort with staging is also evident when they do not have enough microphones, so that certain instruments and certain voices are far too loud, while others remain inaudible. Their shiny costumes covered in tiny mirrors and outlandish sequined hats shaped like churches and pyramids made photo opportunities with them more important to city officials and some audience members than actually hearing their performances.

Coco Raízes's place within the 2004 São João Festival contrasted with that of Reisado das Caraíbas. The group gained access to both the cultural stage and the main stage (named in honor of the group's founder) and built a tourist destination in the neighborhood where the Calixto family lived. Unlike Reisado das Caraíbas, Coco Raízes had been chosen as the representative traditional group of Arcoverde. Although the group members had succeeded in gaining recognition, however, they continued to feel hemmed in by thatch, mud, and palm fronds. The strictures of the genre of traditional music dictate that they must project the image of musical stability, passed down from generation to generation within a happy family. It is a simulacrum of family and community cohesion, of an imagined premodern time when descent mattered more than consent in human relations. Their uniform dress refers to a romanticized pastoral past, contributing to the discursive distancing of the group and relegating it to associations of another era. The percussion and voice arrangements, bereft of any harmonic instruments, also point toward *coco* in Arcoverde as a variety of proto-samba. Coco Raízes are struggling with, and partially emerging from, folklore's assumptions of anonymity and timelessness.

Cordel inspires fans throughout Brazil to go in search of the roots of the band's sounds. Coco Raízes receive these musical tourists and perform these roots. In order for the Calixtos to do this, they must maintain their home base in the margins, far enough but not too far from the capital. When the members of Coco Raízes wanted to move either to Recife or the South as Cordel had done, they were almost universally discouraged by their Recife fans, who reminded them that Arcoverde was their place and that they should stay there.

Cordel's sound and career are grounded by the influence of Coco Raízes and Arcoverde's other traditional music. A regional musical accent provides the band with musical uniqueness in a marketplace perceived as increasingly homogeneous. Cordel signifies "today," and *samba de coco* and *reisado* signify "what came before." The city's layout of the festival follows a logic of spatial and temporal displacement: the cultural stage indexing "here, but not now"; the marginalized and controversial rock stage indexing "now, but not here"; and Cordel at the main stage projecting its stormy version of Arcoverde's "here" and "now" to rebut *forró estilizado*'s saccharine, contemporary regionalism. Gaining access to participate in the modern here and now—rather than being relegated to a nostalgic past or dismissed as not Brazilian enough—is fundamental to the recognition of these musicians' cultural citizenship.

CHAPTER SIX

Tourism

Beginning in the year 2000, after Lula's death raised the profile of the Calixto family, Coco Raízes began to stage performances of varying degrees of formality in the Alto do Cruzeiro neighborhood. Many of these events were planned and promoted by the municipal tourism bureau, with a temporary stage erected next to the cement cross and scenic overlook. Others were more informal *ensaios* (rehearsals), which normally took place in the Calixto Cultural Space or across the street in the Calixtos' bar. By the time I was there in 2004, a steady stream of visitors would come by, a few per week. More would visit on weekends when a performance was planned, either in the bar or at the overlook. The number of visitors surged during the São João Festival and other promoted events, such as the group's birthday celebration each August, which drew several Afro-Brazilian and mestiço northeastern roots groups from Recife and other surrounding areas to perform.

The group's rehearsals proved to be a space of encounter within which the desires and expectations of visitors and musicians were negotiated. When visitors arrived at the Alto do Cruzeiro on a day when a performance was not planned, calls were made to summon the Gomes family up the hill. The visitors were reassured that although a formal performance would not take place that day in Arcoverde, the group would "rehearse," and visitors were welcome to participate. The group downplayed the fact that the rehearsal was taking place, most likely because visitors had arrived—the group had played its repertoire enough that regular rehearsal was not necessary. Throughout these encounters it was unclear to the visitor when the event was planned and choreographed, and when it was merely a glimpse into the group members' spontaneous, music-saturated lives.

On one occasion I stopped by the Calixtos' bar when an elderly couple from Rio de Janeiro were there. His face red with drink, he proclaimed his itinerary driving along the BR-232: "We're going to Triunfo! Serra Talhada! How crazy is that?" They complimented their favorite song from the first CD, and Iram thanked them and began singing it. The woman asked Iram if she had any souvenirs to buy, and she said no, then corrected herself, replying, "Just wooden sandals." They tried on a few pairs of sandals, bought them, and then clapped them together with their hands as they sat and listened to the group sing. At one point the man, obviously drunk, approached Iram and said, stroking her cheek, "You are very beautiful. It's very beautiful, your color." She thanked him gracefully. Iram stood behind the bar, framed by busy, bright floral cloth hanging above the bar, a wooden post, and a bundle of straw that was a leftover decoration for the São João Festival. She began to sing a lullaby that she had written with Lula on his deathbed. Assis, who was sitting at a table with the couple, joined in with the baritone harmony. By the end of the first verse Iuma appeared in the doorway, wearing sweatpants, her hair wet, and started singing the soprano part a parallel third above Iram. Ciço, who had heard the song from the street, rushed in and seamlessly completed the male inner voice so that all four notes rang out. It had the quality of a moment in musical theater when everyone stops and launches into a musical number. The couple from Rio were delighted.

In his writings on tourism, Dean MacCannell (1999) explains how tourism blurs the boundaries between what Erving Goffman terms the "front" and "back" regions. By front and back regions, Goffman is referring to areas clearly available to the public, like a reception area in an office, and areas restricted to authorized personnel, such as a boiler room or a bank vault. This performance by members of Coco Raízes demonstrated the porous nature of the distinction between front and back regions in tourist encounters. The rehearsal was set up as if it would have happened whether the visitors were there or not. It offered a glimpse backstage. Damião Calixto's house is located through the open doorway from the bar; when Iuma appeared, her hair wet after taking a shower, it suggested that the visitor was simply sitting in on a slice of the Calixtos' daily life. At one rehearsal, in the midst of the singing and dancing, Iram's older sister gave her baby a bath in the sink in the corner of the bar. The threshold of authenticity was raised in this warm, intimate, interactive setting. In the words of Kirschenblatt-Gimblett, "an ethnographic bell jar" (1998, 54) was lowered onto the event, and Iram's sister's everyday domestic labor was as much on display as the musicians were.

For visitors willing to dance or play percussion, rehearsals provided an opportunity to interact with the musicians in close proximity. During the rehearsals, the visitors were thrilled to have an unmediated, face-to-face encounter, as opposed to listening to the group's CDs or being separated from Coco Raízes by a stage and PA system. Most visitors adopted the posture of an apprentice, watching and mimicking the dance steps; if they already had some experience, they simply danced along with the rest of the group. Others picked up a *pandeiro* and played along with the songs or asked for pointers regarding technique. Visitors who were well acquainted with the group's repertoire through shows and recordings sang along and requested their favorites. Ciço Gomes improvised verses about the visitors or the scene that he was observing.

There was no obvious boundary between the group and the visitors, yet through the dance, proximity to and distance from the culture bearers was enacted. A standard *samba de coco* song is divided into two parts: a verse with overlapping responsorial singing and a rapid-fire *embolada* section in which a solo singer delivers a stream of notes accented on the strong beats of the 3+3+2 *tresillo* timeline. Two separate dance steps, the *parcela* and the *trupé*, correspond to these two sections. In contrast to the nimble, buoyant steps of urban samba, *samba de coco* is stomped, the steps contributing to layers of percussion sounds, and performers wear wooden sandals called *tamancos* to generate an amplified clapping sound as the wood slaps against the ground. The *parcela* is the initial step that is danced during the verses of the songs. Aligned with the 3+3+2 timeline, it is not as quick as the *trupé*, making it an easier step to learn. With the left foot planted, the right foot stomps twice on the one beat and the and-of-two. The left foot is lifted at the moment when the right foot lands on the and-of-two, and the left lands again on beat four. The right foot generally stomps forward and back, then out to the right and back, tracing an "L" shape, while the left foot remains anchored in the same spot. When the quicker *embolada* section begins, the dancers accelerate their total steps per cycle of the timeline from three to eight, stomping continuously with alternating feet (left-right-left-right . . .) on each pulse and accenting the one and the and-of-two of each measure. In the following diagram, the stressed steps are in uppercase and boldface, while the lighter steps are in lowercase. Each letter represents a pulse, and the periods stand for pulses with no movement.

		3	3	2
Samba de coco timeline		**X..X..X.**		
Parcela		**R..R..L.**		
Trupé		**R**lr**L**rlrl		

As shown, when the verse gives way to the *embolada*, the *parcela* transitions abruptly into the *trupé*, and dancers are suddenly required to move their feet almost three times faster than they have been doing. In the context of the rehearsal, visitors most often reacted to the *trupé* section by attempting to keep up with the steps, while smiling or laughing to indicate that they knew they were faking it and would soon fail. Others simply stayed with the slower *parcela* steps and watched in awe as Fagner and Daiane danced the *trupé* with ease. Inclusion and exclusion were performed through the two dance steps. While the slower *parcela* step was relatively simple to learn, welcoming everyone to participate, the *trupé* sections, especially as *samba de coco* tempos had sped up as the groups professionalized, delineated a line between culture bearer and appreciative, sympathetic audience member. Participation was encouraged, but it was expected that only the culture bearers would be able to do both dance steps with ease.

Trupé dance contests, a staple in Coco Raízes's lengthier performances, also simultaneously downplayed and emphasized sameness and difference. Fans were invited onto the stage to wear wooden sandals, dance *samba de coco*, and be judged by the audience on their dancing competence. Inevitably the audience member did fine during the *parcela* section, but strained to keep up or crashed completely—playing it for laughs—during the *trupé*, providing a basis for the cautionary lyric, "Be careful of your skirt / Because the quick steps are about to start / Stomp the *coco* with care / Beware so that you don't mess up." The audience's missteps were part and parcel of the script of the performance. One day, when I was welcomed into the "back region" of Damião's living room, Iram and Iuma started to do remarkable, spot-on caricatures of the idiosyncratic ways that specific fans danced *samba de coco*. Iram would call out a name, and the two of them would gleefully assume the posture, whether it be hunched over with tiny steps or hopping and flailing their arms before momentarily freezing, coastal *coco*-style. When I danced in the audience at their next performance, it dawned on me that they might do an impression of me in their living room later.

For a well-educated Recife visitor, standing before Fagner and Daiane as they danced the *trupé* steps with the precision of a samba school percussionist is an act of appreciation of local knowledge. In the early 1960s intellectuals such as those in the Paulo Freire–led Movimento de Cultura Popular looked to *coco* and other valuable local knowledge to provide that which illiterate Pernambucans were to bring to the table as part of their dialogic pedagogy. In a similar vein, current *samba de coco* performances are seen as an opportunity to appreciate oral tradition and acknowledge forms of knowledge that many educated urbanites fear they no longer possess. When those possessing more formal education call illiterate and semiliterate musicians who are knowledgeable about oral traditions Mestre (a common practice), the more educated ones are engaging in a drama of the reversal of power relations. This ritual of reversal is often temporary and made unstable by the fact that marginal-turned-traditional musicians' status as bearers of the celebrated folk essence of the region is predicated on a clear differential in social status (in terms of race and class) between fans and musicians. This instability is derived from the tensions inherent in the folklorization of poverty. Within a Left countercultural model that equates civilization with repression, considering its margins to be nooks and crannies where glimmers of freedom still lie, Coco Raízes's visible moves toward middle-class status are precarious.[1] Their upward movement risks deflating the group's folkloric aura, suggesting that group members, too, are living in and therefore alienated by modernity. It then follows that if the group is considered middle class, a musical encounter with them would lose the power to renew an urbanite's "native forces," as Mário de Andrade (1959) phrased it.

Recife ethnomusicologist Cristina Barbosa traces back this particular kind of "ethnomusicological tourism" in the region to the popularity of her ex-boyfriend's band, the Recife roots pop group Mestre Ambrósio. Mestre Ambrósio was formed after the lead singer and instrumentalist Siba spent time outside Recife in the sugar-cane region of the Zona da Mata Norte learning to play the *rabeca*, a kind of folk fiddle. The fiddle had largely been abandoned by the last two generations, and most players at the time (around 1990) were elderly men. Mestre Ambrósio spearheaded a widespread revival of the instrument among high school and college students throughout the Northeast and even into the South. One of their best-known songs, "Pé-de-calçada" (Foot-of-the-sidewalk), recounts their process of going out into rural areas to do musical fieldwork and returning to the city musically energized. One key line, "From the *caboclo*, I know my situation" looks to the Pernambucan interior, in contrast to the *mangue beat* symbol of a satellite dish in the mud, which points outward to the rest of the world.[2]

A quest for an antidote to Recife's mall and high-rise culture is not the only reason visitors come to the Alto do Cruzeiro, however. One local woman's visit to the Alto do Cruzeiro serves as an example of another reason to dance in proximity to Coco Raízes: to accentuate her local distinctiveness in order to stand out in a crowded field of competitors. She was putting together an audition videotape, competing for the honor of being locked into a house under constant televised surveillance together with several strangers on the Globo network's Brazilian version of the popular reality series *Big Brother*. Coco Raízes sang in a semicircle around her as she, clad in a Coco Raízes T-shirt, flopped around in wooden sandals attempting to approximate the *coco* step. After the song stopped she turned to the camera and, in her best diction for television, declared that this group was one of the best things about Arcoverde, and that she was proud that it represented her hometown.

Crepe Ciço Gomes: A Popular Culture–Themed Restaurant

Local musician Helton Moura once told me that he liked to go to events at the Alto do Cruzeiro in order to be a tourist of the tourists, or as he put it, "to go to the zoo to observe the monkeys." He called the Calixtos' bar when tourists visit "Disneyland for people who don't like Disneyland." Helton said that he sometimes felt like yelling angrily at the visitors, especially when he heard young people from Rio say things to each other under their breath like, "Listen to how they talk! How funny!" He felt that these comments revealed their sense that their culture was superior, and this really got under his skin. "What about how funny *they* talk?" he countered. "What about *their* culture? Where do they think we are from? They think we are *matutos* [hicks]."

Helton told me these things as we were seated at another year-round site in Arcoverde that catered to cultural tourism. An upscale restaurant named Casa 21 operated near the center of town in 2004 during my fieldwork year. The ambience and theme of Casa 21 was "local popular culture," one room used as a gallery exhibit space and another as a gift shop selling *coco-* and *reisado*-themed T-shirts and souvenirs. The menu described the place as a "Gastronomical and Cultural Space." Sequined *reisado* hats shaped like churches and pyramids decorated Casa 21. The waitstaff wore satiny, multicolored *reisado* outfits, ribbons streaming from their hats. The menu of the restaurant consisted largely of crepes named after the major families and figures in Arcoverde's music scene. One could order a Crepe Lopes (lemon cream, whipped cream, plum, mint), a Crepe Calixto (dried, salted beef, cream cheese, prato cheese, black pepper, olive oil), a Crepe Ciço Gomes (tuna, ricotta cheese, black olives, cream sauce, sun-dried tomatoes), or a Crepe Rock, a blanket nod to the town's hard rock scene (pineapple, vanilla ice cream, caramel sauce), among other choices (see figure 6.1). According to the owners, the contents of each crepe, and whether it was to be sweet or savory, didn't have any correlation to the personalities of the musicians named, their culinary preferences, or their music. Furthermore, Mestre Horácio, a *reisado* musician who lived in the nearby rural community of Caraíbas—the inspiration for Crepe Mestre Horácio (chicken, bacon, mushroom, cream sauce, rosemary)—was completely unaware that he was featured on the menu when I inquired about it. Naming the crepes after musicians led to the frequent use of the verb *comer*, which in Brazilian Portuguese means "to eat" as well as the slang term "to fuck." This inevitably

04	CREPE REISADO - (atum, creme de queijo, tomate, cebolinha, salsinha)	6,00
05	CREPE CIÇO GOMES - (atum, queijo ricota, azeitona preta, molho, tomate seco)	7,50
06	CREPE SERTÃO - (camarão, molho, mussarela, salsa, tomate seco)	9,00

Figure 6.1. Ciço Gomes crepe at the Casa 21 restaurant (tuna, ricotta, black olives, béchamel sauce, sundried tomatoes). *Photo by the author.*

degenerated into jokes such as, "How many people have eaten Ciço tonight?" During my last week in Arcoverde, the owner named a crepe after me to honor my year studying popular culture. It was quickly proved that I, too, was not immune to receiving these taunts.

A French *forró* band was traveling through the Northeast and had come to Arcoverde to meet Coco Raízes and perform a show one night at Casa 21. Some friends had recommended to the members of the French band that they visit the Alto do Cruzeiro, having spent a week with the Calixtos learning *samba de coco* during the previous year. The female accordion player was technically accomplished at her sparkly black button accordion. She played not only Luiz Gonzaga classics and recent *forró* hits, but also serpentine, choro-influenced melodies full of chromatic ornaments. At certain points she would sing the complex melodies as she played them. The percussionist, sporting a shaved head and goatee, was flashy and very proficient on *pandeiro*, playing variations that I had seen few local players attempt. The sax player alternated between lines that felt *forró*-like and playing that would be better categorized as light jazz/pop. They did their best to put on a show, even though our table made up the entire audience, coaxing us to sing along to Luiz Gonzaga classics. Although I admired their courage in playing *forró* as foreigners in the region where the style emerged, the fragility of the situation struck me. The Arcoverdenses present—Rose Mary and Helton—assumed that the group was going to make a good effort, but ultimately fall short in capturing the *balanço*, or unique lateral swing of *forró*. And perhaps certain stylistic choices, especially in the saxophone, unmasked its playing as "not from around here." But as the set went on, the opposite risk seemed more likely. The accordionist's pristine squeezebox with opalescent inlays was conspicuous in context. Only the top-paid professional Brazilian *forrozeiros* would be able to afford such an instrument. And when she played well—very well—I had the sense that it would have been more reassuring for her not to play so well. If the band members had played badly, it would have been an occasion to pat them on the back for trying, confirming the singularity of the region's music and reinforcing the premise that one had to play it all of one's life to truly play it well. But as they began to play tighter and cleaner than most local *forró* bands, the shiny accordion began to appear more lavish, and the show began to feel to us as it would have if outsiders had gotten on stage and, instead of flailing in an act of self-deprecation, had danced the *trupé* as expertly as Fagner and Daiane. The scene reminded me of a moment when I was singing harmony with Ciço Gomes while visiting his home and he said—in a joking manner with an edge revealing a serious concern—"Oh, no, boy. You're getting too good. You're going to bring those songs home and make loads of money off of us, aren't you?" To Ciço, the fact that my harmonies were not very good reassured him that I did not intend to become famous in the United States as a *samba de coco* singer.

Dreams of a Mud House Tourist Destination

It's a dream. It's a dream that I have. . . . I've been in the group for five years, the entire time wanting to build a headquarters, a cultural store, a cultural inn in Arcoverde for tourists that also serves to host artists for free when they come here to play, at our party, when they come here to pay tribute to what is good, no? A performance space, a stage, for when the tourists arrive we have the means to create an event for them. It's a dream that I have—only money is missing (laughs). It's a big dream.

Iram Calixto

The performance of the French *forró* group and other awkward moments with visitors did not seem to faze the Calixtos. Or if it did bother them, they were consummate professionals and kept their complaints to themselves. Whenever I tried to steer them into talking about whether they thought there was any downside to the visits, they remained firmly on message, committed to their dream of building their own infrastructure to receive tourists. Assis had a vivid picture in his mind's eye of the mud house of his youth. He explained to me the project he envisioned: to re-create the house at the exact site where he lived until he was eight years old, when his family moved to Arcoverde more than fifty years before. He told me about his vision in detail and drew a blueprint. The roof would be made out of dried coconut palm leaves, he explained, insisting that this kind of roof really works—the rain never drips into the house. The door had to be made of vertically aligned sticks, which were removed one by one in order to enter or leave. The window also consisted of sticks, widely spaced like prison cell bars. The bed he pictured was made of sticks woven together with banana leaves. He told me his dream was to realize Lula's unfulfilled dream to do this filming. He wanted to bring Fagner, François, Damião, and the younger male members of Coco Raízes out to the site and spend a couple of days making a documentary film about the process of building the house, making sure that all the details were perfect. The film would end with a big celebration, the whole group dancing *coco* to tamp down the newly built house's dirt floor.

Assis started telling stories from the "old days" of his early childhood. When he was younger than four years old, he said, making himself shake his head and laugh, he wandered off, and it took his mother a while to realize that he was gone. By the time she found him out in the underbrush, he was nursing from a sow, together with a litter of piglets. Another time, he told me, a werewolf came onto their property and circled the house three times, while his mother, terrified, huddled in bed protecting her children. His face lit up as he talked about the old days while tracing the contours of his hand-drawn blueprints for the mud house. When I asked him how many children his mother had raised, he responded in a matter-of-fact manner that he and his three surviving brothers had reached adulthood. The other twelve children had died in early childhood, he added, not including his mother's several miscarriages.

We arranged to go to Rio da Barra a few weeks later. It was the first time Assis had gone back to his childhood home, located sixty kilometers deeper into the *sertão* on the BR-232 highway. I drove him there on a scouting mission to check out how the area had changed and to decide where exactly to build the mud house when he returned with a camera crew to film the construction. Leaving the relatively amenable terrain of the green valley where Arcoverde is nestled, the landscape quickly changed to the *caatinga* scrub brush and cacti.[3] Assis's cousin, who had led the *banda de pífano* at the gazebo during the São João Festival, came along as well, to help us find the right spot. Unlike Assis he had returned to Rio da Barra many times since his childhood. Rose Mary and my friend Nick Arons, who was visiting, tagged along as well.

When Nick first turned on my tape recorder during the car ride, Assis projected his voice into it, adopting a more formal tone, describing his goals for the day as if he were being interviewed on the radio. Soon, however, he relaxed and began telling more stories from his childhood, and soon, as had happened with Severina Lopes in her rocking chair in her front porch/museum, idealized notions of the "old days" gave way to a much more ambivalent portrait of his life in Rio da Barra, the period that he termed the "epoch of mud." This portrait provided occasional glimpses into the trials of everyday life for a poor rural family in the northeastern *sertão*. Most of the anecdotes casually played out in front of a backdrop of hunger and the workings of power between the landowning *coronéis* and the peasants who worked for them.

ASSIS: I wanted to say that this trip of ours to Rio da Barra is really a dream that Lula Calixto had. He wanted to make this documentary of the group, there in Rio da Barra, where we were born. To get to know the place where we were born. But unfortunately, he ended up passing away, and wasn't able to make it happen, so I'm doing this project in his place. So I feel that my life's duty is to realize this dream.

ROSE MARY: How old were you when you came to Arcoverde, Assis?

ASSIS: I arrived when I was eight years old.

DANIEL: And do you remember much from there?

ASSIS: I remember very little—really very little. I do remember the house where we used to live. Yes. I don't remember the area, but I remember what the house was like. Like the furniture. We had a bed made out of branches. The doors were made of sticks. About this, I remember a lot. And the fields of beans and grains that my father would plant.

I also remember when I used to go to the market with him. I was very timid and easily frightened when I was a child. When we saw a soldier, I would hide in between the legs of my father and I wouldn't let him walk. I had the biggest fear of soldiers in the world. These are the kind of reminiscences that it makes me content to be able to talk about today.

ASSIS: I also remember another time, my father went to the market, alone this time. And we all stayed at home, and we didn't have anything, nothing at all. He went to the market, and while he was there, he got in a fight there at the market because of one of our cousins, and he ended up in jail [laughs] because he beat up a guy with a block of raw *sertão* sugar. A big block of raw sugar!

[laughter]

The tough guy took out a knife and Dad picked up the brick of sugar and knocked him upside the guy's head and pow! he fell over. And he ended up in jail. And we were all waiting for him to come back from the market by oxcart with provisions, and there he was in jail!

DANIEL: How long was he in jail?

ASSIS: The next day they let him out. There was a very powerful *coronel* there who was a good friend of my father's. He was the one who got my father out of jail.

At this point in the tape we passed through the small town of Cruzeiro do Nordeste and talked about the last scenes of the film *Central Station*, which were shot there. We strained to remember the town's fictional name, Bom Jesus da Mata, the home of the young, orphaned protagonist Josué. After passing through, Assis piped up with more stories.

ASSIS: There are lots of interesting stories from where we used live, how it was. Other stories, too, because during childhood, my mother used to tell us. But I remember that at a certain age the baby bottle for the children—have you seen a goat's foot bone? She would take that bone and use it as a baby bottle for us kids. A rag, too, and a piece of bone.

ROSE MARY: Tell me, how did she make this?

ASSIS: You wash the bone, and the rag, and . . .

ROSE MARY: The goat's hoof, was it?

ASSIS: No, the anklebone.

DANIEL: It's hollow, then.

ROSE MARY: You take out all of the marrow.

ASSIS: You take a rag. Then you either put milk or tea into the hole in the bone, and stuff the rag down in there, and the kid sucks on the rag.

ROSE MARY: *Meu Deus!*

ASSIS: You did what you had to do, right?

DANIEL: And it worked well?

ASSIS: Look at us now. We're all fat. We're all artists now!

ASSIS: I have another story about my brother. One time, we were at home, and we used to have lots of dogs. We had six dogs. So, what happened? There came a car. A car passed by. Back then, we didn't even know what a train was, we didn't know anything. We didn't know what a doctor was, what a nurse was, what an injection was or any of that kind of stuff. We had heard people talk about them. We heard them talk about them a lot. But to actually see them? So, what happened? This car ran over one of our dogs, and we, we were young at the time, we all started to cry because we felt so sorry for this dog. Then, finally, Lula said to me: "Hey, I remember! I've heard about this thing called an injection!" Now, my father, he used to make sandals out of strips of leather, bandit's sandals. So, what happened, then? There was a tool made to puncture leather, and my brother had heard of an injection, so he said "Oh yeah, I'm going to get that tool to give the dog an injection so that he can get better." Now, this iron tool, when it pierced the dog's neck it ended up killing the poor thing!

When we arrived in Rio da Barra, Assis exclaimed, "Here really is the *sertão*! The tough, brutal *sertão*." Assis's cousin, who had reached a verbose stage

Figure 6.2. Assis surveys the moon-scape-like terrain where his childhood home used to stand. *Photo by the author.*

of drunkenness before the drive even began, cried, "These are my people! Here, they're all family! This is my place!" From the dirt road there was no indication that there had been a house on this piece of rocky desert. A large, pockmarked slab of rock lent a moonscape-like appearance to the terrain, as a vulture circled nearby.

Assis surveyed the landscape and found a small mound of dirt that was once his family's house (see figure 6.2). He recognized the plants first: "Here is *alastrado*.[4] Oftentimes, during the droughts, when we didn't have anything else to eat, we would eat this cactus. To cook it, you just had to take the spiny layer off of it, and take out the pulp at its core. Then you can eat it."

After walking around the moonscape for a few minutes, talking about the names of the plants, the rocks, and the hill in the distance where his cousin had grown up, we returned to the car to go back to Arcoverde. On the way back Assis reminisced about the hardships his family faced: "It was a hugely difficult life. It was so difficult there that it was necessary for us to leave, because there wasn't any way to live. My father said, 'No, I'm not going to let my kids die here.' There was no work for him. It was in 1952 that he said, 'no, it's time for us to go.' We moved to Arcoverde and my father started to work in the Celpe digging holes for electrical poles. I think I have a photograph of him, erecting electrical poles."[5]

When we arrived back in Arcoverde Assis made a closing statement for the day, assuming his radio voice once more: "And now we are returning from my birthplace, and I was pretty emotional, because when I left here, I left as a young, little kid, but my desire was to get reacquainted with the place where I was born, to step on the earth where my old house once stood, and also to do this project—doing Lula Calixto's work—God willing. We're going to return. I'm going to try to nail down the date for us to return. I'd like to do it before Daniel goes away, and he's going away soon."

Assis had returned to the piece of land where he grew up for the first time in order to plan a documentary film in which his family would rebuild his childhood home. In his plan, Coco Raízes would compact the dirt floor of the replica of the mud house with a thatched roof, creating a site to concretize the link between the *samba de coco* dance and the family's rural *sertão* roots. The site would serve as a tourist party destination less than an hour outside of Arcoverde, and the documentary film/music video would promote both the group and the destination. This trip, spurred by his brother's dream and the mud house replicas in the staged village at the São João Festival, inspired Assis to remember stories from his past in Rio da Barra. But despite the dream, the blueprint, the secured funding, and the scouting mission, Assis never mentioned the Rio da Barra project to me again. Neither the mud house nor the film ever materialized. Although he never explicitly told me why he dropped the idea, our visit to the barren site that day appears to have been the turning point leading to his change of heart.

When he used his radio voice, he presented his nostalgia in a more straightforward fashion, as a representative of the group doing public relations work. But as the drive continued, his relationship to the past in his stories became more complex. The stories he remembered indexed hunger, fear, and a sense of powerlessness in the face of the state. The harrowing, macabre tale of Lula's fruitless attempt to save his dog presents a vision of a rural past located not outside of modernity, but inside it, helplessly subject to its dangers while being excluded from access to its powerful knowledge and technology. In this way Assis's anecdotes stand in stark contrast to the Globo network's depiction of rural *sertão* life as a wholesome, carefree celebration.

A Jazzman's Plans for Coco Raízes

Before the Rio da Barra rebuilding plan fell through, the US jazz drummer Andrew Potter had offered to pay for the documentary chronicling the project. I was interested in Potter's impulse to support the band financially, asking myself several questions: What did Coco Raízes mean to him? What about them inspired him so much? What kind of professional relationship did he expect to have with them? Potter's relationship to Coco Raízes was just one of many relationships the band was developing with contacts in the music industry who could help it record, tour, and promote itself. Potter had links to musicians in Chicago, providing the group with its first projection outside of Brazil. During 2004 the group's career began to gather steam, both nationally and internationally, and the Potter-financed second recording *Godê Pavão* played a role in this success. Two European compilation CDs included the song "Godê Pavão," and French producer Marc Regnier paid Coco Raízes a visit to discuss signing them to a European tour and international CD distribution deal on his record label Outro Brasil (Other Brazil).[6] Marc had already taken Cordel and several other Pernambucan acts on tour to Europe and Japan and helped release their recordings internationally. Coco Raízes, who up to this point had a career overwhelmingly based on performances within Pernambuco, were on the cusp of attaining a more global reach for their CD distribution and touring. Detailing how Potter views the group offers a glimpse of how the group may be seen outside Brazil.

Andrew Potter and Assis spoke regularly on the phone, especially when Potter was at his house in southern Brazil. After hearing Potter's version of Assis's song and learning about his involvement with Coco Raízes, I searched online to see what information was available about his career. He had recorded with various jazz and jazz fusion groups since the 1970s. It turned out that Potter was a frequent poster on the public forum at jazz artist Branford Marsalis's Web site. Following is a selection of posts that appear to have been written hastily, perhaps to keep up the conversational rhythm on a combative Internet message board on which bragging, posturing, and insults were standard practices:

> i want to take the time on the branford marsalis forum to announce that since 1996, i have slowly evolved a new way to express pulse in the rhythm section. There are three basic influences, and, jazz is a serious part, but, is not the only part. It's important to note, the jazz doesn't water down in the mixture, it actually expands from where it is at now. The first influence is the mangue beat sound of Recife, Pernambuco. Chico Science and Nação Zumbi, Coco Raiz do Arcoverde, Nação Pernambuco are just some of the incredible sounds coming from there, they changed my outlook of how i could express rhythm with more power and possibility. . . . so, INNOVATION thilo, is it possible for jazz in our lifetime?

This post establishes Potter's claim to being inspired and influenced by Afro-Pernambucan sounds such as *mangue beat*'s mixture of Afro-diasporic sounds with Afro-Pernambucan styles of maracatu and *coco*. According to Potter, his musical innovation within the jazz world, which he calls "mangue jazz," is a new way of incorporating the rhythmic elements of *coco* and maracatu into jazz drumming. For Potter, Pernambucan sounds such as *coco* provide an essential mark of distinction separating his music from previous styles of jazz:

> . . . i just heard the finished master of a folclorico group i helped produce, coco raiz do arcoverde, a fantastic group of the dance and rhythm they call coco. it

is an extremely simple and beautiful call response type music, with melodies i haven't heard in any popular brazilian music.

For Potter, *samba de coco*'s simplicity is the group's virtue. The group's uniqueness attracted him to journey deep within the heart of a faraway, exotic place ("it was like i had gone to the khyber pass") and bring with him the sounds of jazz to present them for the first time:

> i went to arcoverde, invited by them after they read in the jornal do commercio that i liked them, i brought the first jazz group to arcoverde, a city in the interior of pernambuco, the state of brazil, a taxi driver told me later on that it was like i had gone to the kyber pass, and, i was mesmerised by the dance and rhythm. many people might think *coco* is too simple, but, i am always putting it on after some jazz listening, and, it just grooves me out. it is an important part of mangue jazz, as is the dance and rythm and tradition of maracatu. it is older than jazz or samba, some records go back as far as 300 years, and, you know that kind of hitch step you see in those guys with the new orleans marching jazz bands? well, i see that kind of step in a maracatu procession. it is very powerful stuff, and, i'd be happy to go into detail for anyone who wants to ask. i can hang on this thread a long time just talking about experiences you all haven't had.

The tropes of expedition, discovery, and the exchange of cultural riches have proven enduring in the New World, and Potter's variation on this theme carries with it some characteristic narrative silences.[7] As Steve Feld points out in his article on the use of sounds from Central African field recordings in avant-garde pop and jazz, jazz musicians, whether black or white, generally consider the "bounds of mimesis"—the rules delineating the imitable—to be wide open. Such imitation is most often seen as "in the tradition" (Feld 1996, 9). In fact, this process of citation/mimesis/copying is not generally thought of as theft, but as a source of the genre's revitalization. Feld also points out that jazz has long celebrated parts of Africa without necessarily seeking a direct historical connection (ibid.). The reference to New Orleans is telling, as it makes a parallel between Pernambuco and the US city synonymous with the roots of jazz.[8] For Potter, jazz is on the skids, and "discovering" Pernambuco as a new musical reservoir, a new New Orleans, is the answer to stopping its downward spiral.

Potter even has an ambitious plan to carry out this resurrection. He pitched a movie to Marsalis in which Marsalis would play a jazz musician and Halle Berry his love interest, a dancer from Recife. In the story Marsalis's character receives a grant to go to Recife and study Pernambucan music. While there, he meets Berry, who takes him to see groups such as Coco Raízes and Maracatu Nação Pernambuco. Potter proposes to make both a Hollywood film and an HBO made-for-TV movie, suggesting that they push the violence and danger of being in Brazil. When he returns to Chicago he brings Berry with him, and she helps create a new dance craze on the south side of the city. The climax of the movie is Marsalis and his partners somehow battling a racist and his gang, with a *mangue beat* soundtrack. The pitch ended with "the new dances could inject something fresh in american culture and tie jazz back in with dancing."

Potter's pitch offers a revealing script of how *samba de coco* inspires him and fits into his plans to revitalize jazz. In this narrative Coco Raízes are a bit of the African diaspora located on the receding frontier of the untouched. They are a supplier of authenticity and of invigorating rhythms and dance steps to be discovered, exported, and honed into jazz. The allure and the danger of the exotic are to be exploited together, because that's what it takes to make it in Hollywood.

What does this script do? By framing *coco* as a musical elixir healing jazz (as well as a tonic to boost both Marsalis's and Potter's careers), it obscures the Calixto family's complex, ongoing engagement with modernity, which reaches back beyond Assis, Lula, and Damião to their father, who moved to the city to make a living erecting electrical poles. It treats Coco Raízes as an emblem of the survival of the past in the present, a raw cultural nugget just waiting to be mined, improved, and made contemporary. It projects the use of wooden sandals, a coastal *coco* practice adopted in Arcoverde in the mid-1990s, back into a primordial past. This process also obscures the ongoing musical transformation that took place through the decades, as Biu Neguinho transferred to his *coco* beats the knowledge of percussion that he had accrued directing a Rio-style samba school in Arcoverde for several years.[9] This script willfully ignores the group's musical changes over the previous decade of professionalizing: (1) the honing of the vocals; (2) the rising tempos; (3) the shifting configuration of the stage show, from twenty-five to thirty people dancing on stage to two or three; (4) the miking and amplification of the sandals on plywood; and (5) the shift to an almost exclusively new repertoire of original songs, among other changes.

Potter's ready-made slot for *coco*, however, should not be seen as the dominant script narrating Coco Raízes's entrance into the musical marketplace.[10] Potter attempts to fit them into a decades-old story of the next Latin dance craze, but he does not fully succeed; Marsalis did not even acknowledge Potter's post, let alone take him up on the offer. Neither did the other interested parties involved in Coco Raízes's career reduce the group's story in such a drastic way. Although Coco Raízes maneuver within scripts such as Potter's and Mestre Ambrósio's updated version of Mário de Andrade's trek, the group is not completely contained by them. Within this network of individual and institutional power brokers (who are attracted to Coco Raízes for a variety of motives), the group is making more and more decisions about its own production. By utilizing alliances with intermediaries such as Potter, Cordel's producer Gutie, Cordel's French tour manager Marc Regnier, and the Globo Network, Coco Raízes have been able to rise within the roots music circuit and into world music circulation. As I was preparing to return to the United States in September 2004, Regnier signed the group for European distribution of their CD and a tour.

While preparing for this tour, Carlinhos, their stage manager and sound engineer, came to me and asked me to use my laptop computer to chop up an old cassette recording of Lula and the group from the mid-1990s. Carlinhos had a plan to begin the group's shows in Europe with a videotape showing images of Lula Calixto and wanted the group to sing live backup harmonies to the recording of Lula's lead vocal. At his request I removed the background vocals and as much of the low frequencies of the percussion as possible, compressing and equalizing Lula's voice to isolate and emphasize it. Carlinhos insisted, however, that I leave the cassette noise intact—"cru" (raw), in his words—in order to foreground the recording's status as an artifact of the group's past. He preferred that I not tell the rest of the group as I performed these edits. He was still trying to figure out the best way to convince the performers to accept the technology-based innovation.

Around the time of their trip to France, Assis wrote a song that quickly became a new favorite for the group and fans alike. It is called "O Medroso" (The frightened one). He wrote it while thinking about his upcoming first plane ride only a few years after the attacks on September 11, 2001:

> I don't go by plane
> It's very dangerous
> I only go by old car
> It's much more enjoyable

> *Não ando de avião*
> *Que é muito perigoso*
> *Só ando de carro velho*
> *Muito mais gostoso*

Assis's catchy refrain reminded me of another passage from Câmara Cascudo's 1937 love letter to the *sertão*: "Also rare is the place in the *sertão* that hasn't been flown over by a plane. The bandit is acquainted with very modern automatic weapons. He likes silk socks, perfumes. Some have polished nails. . . . Almost all of them wear 'cowboy' outfits, big, worn-out leather hats, side arms, handkerchief around their necks. The handkerchief around the neck, as artists from Rio de Janeiro 'represented' hicks in the Northeast, is a purely theatrical influence. No one wears this here in the Northeast. If someone rolls up a handkerchief and wears it around his neck, it's because he is sick" (2004, 12).

I made the return trip from Arcoverde to Recife to catch a plane to São Paulo to spend a day with Cordel before returning to Texas. Riding on the bus, I cursed the fact that the potholes near Caruaru that had jackhammered my car for so many months had finally been repaired, just in time for my leaving. I thought about how, besides Assis's new song, there were other examples in the music of Coco Raízes and Cordel in which the lyrics about transportation and leaving stood in contrast to their circumstances. Ciço sang, "I'm going to the South to make some money," as he stayed in the *sertão*. Lirinha countered, "My people, don't go away on the Itapemirim [long-distance bus]," because the rain was about to fall, making crops grow.[11] Ironically, although Cordel wrote the song "Chover (ou Invocação para um dia líquido)" [Rain (or Invocation for a Liquid Day)] when its members still lived in Arcoverde, the song's success helped spur their decision to go away to the South to develop their careers.

I flew from Recife to São Paulo and stayed with Lirinha and Bolinho, Micheliny Verunschk's boyfriend, who worked as Cordel's sound engineer. The stopover ended up being shorter than twenty-four hours. Lirinha and Bolinho had rented a house together, while the drummers Emerson, Nego Henrique, and Rafa Almeida all shared a small room with three twin beds in a row in a hotel on a busy São Paulo street. The drummers were regulars at the hotel, living out of their suitcases in a different room each time they returned from touring.

While Lirinha was out of the house much of the day, Bolinho kept me busy, showing me some of the new sound montages that he was piecing together for their upcoming tour. Zé do Né's a capella cowherder's melody hovered between the left and right speakers, combined with sounds from a German subway, recorded on their European tour. The samples melted into a disorienting, swirling dream on the speakers, but on the computer screen they appeared more orderly. The seams between the audio clips were evident, and zigzagging vectors in primary colors directed a choreography of volume changes and stereo panning. Bolinho also cross-faded into the mix what appeared to be sounds of an amusement park. He listed the sources of many of the sound effects heard on Cordel's recordings. The sounds of horses panicking in the riot at the beginning of "Vou Saquear a Tua Feira" (I'm going to loot your market) were sampled from a battle scene in a

Hollywood movie. The thunder sounds, however, were his, he told me. He had held a microphone out a window during an especially dramatic storm.

Micheliny stopped by to visit her boyfriend and check on me. She had moved from Arcoverde to São Paulo a few months before, started a graduate degree in literature, and found a job at Itaú Cultural, one of the foremost cultural foundations in the country. Micheliny loved São Paulo. She told me about her new book, for which she had already written four chapters. It is about a suicidal saint and the havoc this wreaks on the Catholic Church's hierarchy. One of the characters is an ambitious bishop who needs the saint's death in order to be promoted to pope. The fourth chapter is about the history of a cemetery. In it, Micheliny explained, she compares reality shows to cemeteries, museums to cemeteries, and literature to a cemetery.

I was finally able to sit down and formally interview Lirinha right before I had to leave for the airport. Responding to my first question regarding how the Northeast is viewed, he impressed upon me how the task of the performer resembles the task of the researcher by immediately referring to two academic texts I was using to understand northeastern musical regionalism:

> I believe that this whole thing of glorifying a place, generates the invention of a place that is diverse and multiple by nature. For example, Recife, in the case of Recife. . . . [T]he music that the majority of the population likes isn't the *mangue* movement. Yes, but there is this invented idea that what is bubbling up in Recife is *mangue* musicality. This invention, and I use the word invention derived from a book called the *Invention of the Northeast* . . . and also, later, I also had a book that I think you know called *The Mystery of Samba* by Hermano Vianna.[12] They touch upon two ideas of invention.
>
> Why did I mention this? First, I came to understand this idea of invention based on my travels through the country, and a series of interviews that I gave where I had to satisfy people's curiosities regarding a fictitious Northeast. I realized that this invention was by a literary movement, the movement of Jorge Amado, João Cabral de Melo Neto, Raquel de Queiroz, Graciliano Ramos called regionalism. And even today our music earned the label of *música regional* based on the propagation of an intellectual idea of what it is to be a northeasterner.
>
> I completely disagree with this because there is a vision, an invention, that the Southeast of Brazil is up-to-date, futurist, modern and the Northeast is archaic, retrograde, conservative, right?

He spoke deliberately, varying the emphasis of his words and savoring their pronunciation, with an echo of the preacher's cadence that he projected on stage. I was adjusting to hearing his voice live, next to me, which was jarring after listening carefully to his vocal tracks on CD for so long. His voice at a conversational volume was familiar yet distinct from Cordel's recordings. Lirinha's interpretations of Arcoverde intricately overlapped with and detoured from my own preliminary reflections on the last year. He was frank about Cordel's marketing goal of citing Arcoverde to avoid being overshadowed within the *mangue beat* scene and how at that moment, in São Paulo, this strategy had become a burden for his career:

So in the first phase of Cordel do Fogo Encantado—I wouldn't hide it at all— we used the Arcoverde thing a fair amount. Not in a sleazy way, but yes, we did. We talked a lot about Arcoverde to distinguish ourselves from the *mangue* movement from Recife. That we were from the *sertão*. . . . [I]t was fruitful, I think, for the city. I think that it wasn't negative. But now I realize that it places us in a prison, a jail cell, handcuffs that are very cruel in this place [São Paulo] within the country . . .

. . . Because, in order to understand this whole process, I think it is important to understand that we're in a capitalist world of capitalist human relations. So, when a city begins to have musical products, more than one, interesting products in the marketplace, original products, never before seen, and all, an aura starts to form around this place that is different from other places.

. . . And this other thing starts to surface also, a worldwide phenomenon I think: a response to globalization. Because globalization is dialectical like that. It happened in the nineties. Globalization in the sense of homogeneity of products, homogenous things. Tribal screams started to surge forth. Yes, it was like that. It was very much like that at the time.

Lirinha's voice rose in intensity as he spoke of the weight of the associations of percussion and oral tradition with the ancestral or primitive, arguing that recent additions and transformations within *samba de coco* had quickly become seen as age-old traditions:

[Coco Raízes] dressed in drag, you know, in costume as a traditional thing, with all the cultural baggage of everything that is percussive, enchanted, and oral, and they're black—it's "ancestral." But, there are various recently included symbols and elements that people don't have the courage to mention so as not to crumble every romantic notion that has been created around *coco*. The surdo drum, that is now considered traditional, was taken up in the decade of the sixties. For me, that's more recent than some Rolling Stones records. The sandals are a thing that came with Fundarpe, that already had a vision of *coco* as beach *coco* that used the sandals.

Lirinha inverted the negative valence of the word *descaracterizado* (meaning defaced or rendered unrecognizable), a term usually employed to dismiss a purportedly traditional practice that was, according to the strictures of folklore, being deformed or abused through the corrupting contact of modernity:

I saw *coco*, I lived *coco* in Arcoverde in situations that I thought were great. I really enjoy things that are *descaracterizadas*. I see in *descaracterização*, you know, the real oxygen of things. In adaptations.

I remember one time Lula Calixto was in sneakers, and there was a photographer from the magazine *Veja*. It was at opening night of the film *Central do Brasil* and Lula was there playing the *pífano*. And Lula's *pífano* is made of PVC pipe, not bamboo. And the guy approached to take a picture. "Man," he told me, "that business isn't traditional, it's all *descaracterizado*. I didn't take the picture."

I interjected, "He didn't take the picture?" and Lirinha shook his head and said, "The flute wasn't bamboo, the guy was in sneakers." Our interview was cut short when the taxi arrived to drive me to the airport. On the flight back I took out my laptop and started fussing with the rough mix of a song that I had recorded for Alberone Padilha and his roots group Tabocas de Ouro. As I calibrated volume levels, I thought about the day a few weeks before when I had turned my apartment into a recording studio, cramming Iram Calixto, Iuma Calixto, Helton, Rose Mary, and other Bar do Zaca regulars into a small bedroom to sing a chorus. Alberone had written a buoyant anthem to Arcoverde, a midtempo *xote* with flute; saxophone; whistling; and a riot of drums, *pandeiro,* shakers, bells, and marching band cymbals that evoked a carefree parade. When I played it back for him right after we recorded the tracks, he expressed a desire that someday it would be blasted from the speaker trucks to promote the São João Festival. Listening to the rough mix on the plane, at certain moments I could pick individual voices out of the ad hoc chorus assembled that afternoon. I listened to it over and over, tweaking the mix, until the laptop battery ran out.

THE LAND OF BRAZIL

I am
I am from South America, yes
I was born here, as I am from here, you see
Brazil is my place

Northeast, east, west and southeast
It's the land of tough old goats
Brazil is my place

I feel *saudade*
If I'm not here, you see
As the place where I emerged, yes
Has *agreste* and has *sertão*

It has virgin forest
Nature, Indians
Satellite dishes and VCRs
In this place I'm going to stay

Arcoverde, piece of Pernambuco
You can make it through more years still
You're part of Brazilian America

Humble people
Good-hearted folks
That are part of this nation
Of this great and rich land

TERRA BRASIL

Alberone Padilha

Eu sou
Sou da América do sul, sim
Nasci aqui, pois sou daqui, viu
O Brasil é o meu lugar

Nordeste, leste, oeste e sudeste
É terra de cabra da peste
O Brasil é o meu lugar

Sinto saudade
Se eu não estou aqui, viu
Pois o lugar que eu surgi, sim
Tem agreste e tem sertão

Tem mata virgem
Natureza, Indio
Parabólica e vídeo
Nesse lugar eu vou ficar

Arcoverde, pedaço de Pernambuco
Pode entrar ainda mais ano
É do Brasileiro America

Gente humilde
Povo de bom coração
Que faz parte da nação
Dessa terra grande e rica

CHAPTER SEVEN

Elegy

Upon returning to Austin, Texas, my wife Laura and I displayed on our walls, clipped to clipboards, some eight-by-ten-inch photographs of Assis Calixto, Ciço Gomes, and other musicians from Arcoverde. After we put them up we joked that they were my "specimens," acknowledging the critique of the ethnographer as butterfly collector. Quickly, however, it struck me that it wasn't possible to will away the complications of writing about people while living so far away from them. This is a problem that stems from the timeline of travel grants, graduate assistantships, and teaching positions within this particular academic trajectory. It often felt disjointed to spend my days thinking, writing, and teaching about one place while living in another. I admit, however, that I enjoyed the focus that I found in the long, empty, sterile, white room of study carrels on the second floor of the Benson Latin American Collection at the University of Texas at Austin. The spiraling consequences of moments of friendship and ethnography between Lula Calixto and Lirinha in a Northeast region cloaked in nostalgia were proving complicated to make sense of, and the stillness aided my concentration.

As I wrote I continued to stay in touch with people in Arcoverde—Rose Mary and Micheliny in particular—and would hear about the successes of, ongoing conflicts between, and tragedies befalling Arcoverde's musicians. A photo of Coco Raízes in front of the Eiffel Tower proved that their European tour came through after all; Micheliny Verunschk moved to São Paulo to pursue her career as a poet and prose writer after a book of her poems was nominated for the prestigious Portuguese Telecom literary prize; and Ciço Gomes, feeling that his crucial role as the group's only vocal improviser was being taken for granted, left the group several times only to return, daunted by the prospect of building up a new group's reputation and visibility. I received the devastating news that Pastor, the charismatic lead singer of the band Cobaias (Guinea Pigs), had hanged himself, leaving the black-shirted teenagers who so fiercely admired him desperately wondering why. The older Lopes sister, Lení, also passed away, and the feud between the two rival *samba de coco* groups had subsided by the time the 2005 São João Festival came around, when the municipal government gave a better-rehearsed and more confident Lopes family *coco* group ample opportunities to perform on the rural-themed cultural stage. News, both encouraging and discouraging, circulated in both directions. My dissertation committee chair, Gerard Béhague, with whom I had worked for seven years, died a few months after I returned, just as I had begun to write.

One exciting piece of news was that Cordel had been selected as a featured group in the opening ceremonies for the 2007 Pan-American games. It was held in the enormous Maracanã Stadium in Rio de Janeiro for a capacity crowd of around ninety thousand and television viewers all across the Americas. Cordel lip-synched its medley of a *foguete de roda* song, learned from Coco Raízes, and a traditional *reisado* song, learned from Reisado das Caraíbas. The group performed on top of an elaborate, wedding-cake-like circular stage surrounded by a series of spiraling ramps, with hundreds of costumed figures from the folklore of various Brazilian regions scurrying around below, lighting up the scene with enormous sparklers. Here is how the Globo network television announcers described it: "It is as if night has fallen, and all of our fears have arrived. In an enormous chair sits a very, very small person. The size of the chair makes them look quite fragile, quite scared. They are all folkloric manifestations that have to do with our fears . . . many things from Brazilian folklore: boi bumbá, bumba meu boi, various manifestations. Ciranda, the Saint's day festivals in June."

Glittering *caboclo-de-lança* warriors from *maracatu rural*, revelers dressed as the harlequin Mateus from *reisado*, and huge twenty-foot-tall puppets as featured in Olinda's Carnaval danced below the wedding cake stage. On top a bewildered Cordel, in carefully chosen contemporary "street" clothes, struggled to keep up with its own taped sounds echoing through the enormous stadium. At key moments in the *foguete de roda*—a São João genre of quick duple time marches whose name means "firecracker in the round"—an elaborate display of fireworks exploded in time along the perimeter of the stadium. As the song came to a close, the identical Mateuses mimed a prerecorded fanfare on long horns and proceeded to string maypole-like ribbons from the top of the stage to the ground below.

My initial reaction to the spectacle was to count it as firm evidence that despite Cordel's best efforts to escape the confines of folklorism, the risk is always present that the group members will be marked as traditional culture bearers of the Northeast and forced to operate within the strictures of folkloristic staging. Yet this particular performance was complicated by the way in which the northern and northeastern cultural forms were imbricated in what appears to be a strangely Freudian national allegory. Unlike the asceticism of folkloric performance, in which performers strive to downplay artifice and present their playing as part of a "slice of life," this ceremony is a lavish spectacle that represents an officially sanctioned performance of the nation for an audience of the rest of Latin America, the Caribbean, and to a lesser extent, Anglophone North America. Cultural forms and practices from outside the Southeast Rio/São Paulo axis, most of which are usually performed during celebrations, are narrated as manifestations of fear. The event's director adopted an oddly psychoanalytical approach to the representation of national folklore. Regionally peripheral others within Brazil's uneven development are framed as the contents of what Freud conceived of as the unconscious id. Members of Cordel, in contrast, dressed in contemporary clothes and performing traditional tunes, danced on the top of the wedding cake–shaped stage, occupying a mediating role between the anonymous folkloric manifestations dancing under them and the contemporary MPB artists with whom they shared the bill.

The Cordel drummer Emerson Calado disagreed with this assessment, however. When I spoke to him about the experience, he responded positively, excited to have been able to participate in such an enormous production. He was thrilled that President Lula da Silva was in attendance and that it had been viewed by an unimaginably large number of people live and on television. The director was a fan of the band and knew its repertoire well. He choreographed the spiraling fireworks so that they would coordinate with the *foguete de roda* song and would match the circular movement of the maypole ribbons. Emerson's only regret was that in the television broadcast the editors missed opportunities to highlight that moment visually through the bird's-eye view camera mounted on a helicopter.

After finishing graduate school and moving around the United States for a couple of one-year teaching positions, I landed in New Orleans, a city that occupies a similar place in the US national imaginary as Pernambuco does in Brazil: as a postplantation repository of folklore and tradition that relies on tourist income and struggles economically despite its storied history. As I settled into a longer-term academic position in Louisiana, I was able to return to the São João Festival in Arcoverde to see what it had become.

When I returned to Brazil I noticed both changes and continuities in the festival. It had been four years since the Zeca Cavalcanti administration had replaced the previous mayor, Rosa Barros, yet the festival continued to be structured more or less the same way that it had been earlier. At the epicenter stood, once again, a reenactment of the town's beginnings, and spread out around the staged village were various stages featuring glitzy *forró es-tilizado*, roots *forró pé-de-serra*, *samba de coco*, and rock, and straddling these genres, Cordel do fogo Encantado. The number of visitors had increased, and mud constructions had proliferated. Whereas before there were only three small mud huts in the staged village, mud was covering bars, food vendors, stores selling handicrafts, and even a tourist information center. Interestingly, the church at the center of the staged village, which had been made of painted plywood before, was re-created half a decade later out of mud. The staged village was separated from the nearest road by a crop of cornstalks standing more than four feet tall, which art director Suedson had planted a couple of months before. The mud huts, mud church, and corn provided photo ops for festivalgoers, who would pose even in front of the tourist information center for a rustic backdrop to accompany their celebration of the harvest season.

The festival kept nocturnal hours, activity swelling and subsiding between 10:00 pm and 5:00 am. Located in the center of the city, it created a São João soundscape that beckoned (and repelled) residents, radiating out toward the outskirts, reminding all within earshot that the municipal government was actively invested in throwing them a huge party. In addition to the planned performances, spontaneous additions to the festival's soundscape surfaced as well. The most audible was triggered when the news of Michael Jackson's sudden death spread through the festival the day after São João's Day proper. Spontaneous singalongs of "Billy Jean" and "Beat It" added to the cacophony, and sound trucks loaded with speakers drove through the city blaring the international king of pop's once again ubiquitous hits.

The festival's honored guests were Reisado das Caraíbas. The façade of the main stage was shaped like the distinctive church-shaped hat worn by a key *reisado* dancer. Billboards sponsored by a health insurance plan featured the elderly performers in their glittery, multicolored dress with the caption "Live your life with Unimed," prominently placed on the façade of the VIP rooms lining the avenue (see figure 7.1). Life-sized wooden figures of the three kings stood in front of the mud church. By this point the Reisado das Caraíbas had achieved a level of success that had eluded them in 2004: they had been invited to Recife to participate in an official Christmas celebration and had been invited by Itau Bank to participate in a recording project and tour throughout Brazil. Their place of honor at the center of the festival—the very place where Coco Raizes had stood in 2004—reinforced how interchangeable, fleeting, and unstable this sort of symbolic social inclusion by the municipal government was. In certain ways their role felt like that of a logo or mascot.

The uneasy coexistence of marginal-turned-traditional musicians' privileged role in the festival and the municipal government's disregard for the

Figure 7.1. The Reisado das Caraíbas featured on a sign advertising a health-care plan. Zezé, in his signature pyramid hat, is featured in the back. *Photo by the author.*

welfare of the socially marginal was evident in another striking addition to that year's festival. Along with rows of actual corn planted and a proliferation of mud, twelve life-sized marionettes of the members of the Reisado dangled from large trees near the staged village. As I approached this area, they immediately struck me as eerie. This was a life-sized diorama that depicted living musicians as silent, poseable dolls, immediately bringing to mind a taxidermic mode of cultural representation. The mannequins featured detachable, segmented wooden limbs with no knees or elbows. Their heads and hands were made of papier-mâché, and although they were crafted in a rough-hewn, folksy style, it was evident that Suedson and his team had put an incredible amount of painstaking work into creating and stringing up the sculptures. Each stood in its own unique pose, stomping the *reisado* steps, looking over at another dancer, and diligently playing the triangle, and no barrier existed separating the tableau from the rest of the staged village. Festivalgoers stopped and posed for pictures alongside the marionettes, some even putting their arms around the shoulders of one of the large dolls. I became curious about what attracted people to the scene and began to take my own pictures, both of the mannequins and of others' picture taking. In my photos a boy around ten years old clutches one of the female dancers, pulling her close as if to dance *forró*, his hand resting on the small of the mannequin's back. In another a woman sidles close to the accordion player and pretends to play the instrument along with the papier-mâché musician. In each of the pictures the festivalgoers find pleasure in exhibiting camaraderie with the marionettes.

While I was taking pictures of the picture takers, Zezé found me. The dancer who represents the Moors within the Reisado, Zezé is the only one who wears a pyramid hat decorated with mirrors and sequins. All of the Reisado members lived relatively humble lives, but Zezé, a subsistence farmer who supplemented his income by making wicker baskets and brooms, was clearly the poorest in the group. He described himself as a *caboclo*, a rural person with a mixture of indigenous and Afro-Brazilian features, and Arc-overdenses would identify his dark skin and face as such. He had walked three hours to the festival when he learned that I had returned to the city. When he first saw the marionettes, he gazed at them, standing and watching several visitors stop and pose for a picture with his avatar. He lingered by the mannequins wearing his pyramid hat. But most of the picture takers preferred Zezé's papier-mâché doppelgänger to the man himself. Unlike with Zezé the man, they wouldn't have to break the ice with Zezé the marionette, gauging whether or not he was friendly. A few festivalgoers asked if they could borrow his hat to wear for their pictures with the dolls. At one point two girls approached him and asked if they could have a picture taken with him wearing his hat. A series of pictures I took that night chronicled these and other moments: Zezé looking straight into the camera with his arms around two of the mannequins; Zezé wearing his pyramid hat, the fishing line strung from the trees at an angle that made it look as though it was also holding him in place (see figure 7.2).

The Unraveling of Cordel and Coco Raízes

In retrospect, knowing that the 2009 São João performance would be Cordel's last, I saw telltale signs that the band's days were numbered. The latest alteration in its sound was the addition of a bass player and a trombone and euphonium player. Both were highly skilled players, but this change, after the group had defended its unique nylon-string guitar and heavy percussion format for a decade, seemed an attempt to compensate for a loss of momentum and creative direction. In many places the show was louder, darker, and more claustrophobic than previous performances I had attended. The addition of the bass made these stormy moments feel

Figure 7.2. Zezé stands with the life-sized marionettes of his bandmates.
Photo by the author.

more like conventional, riff-driven heavy rock than Cordel's earlier work, in which songs matched rock intensity but assiduously avoided rock conventions and the typical rock lineup of drumset, bass, electric guitar, and vocals. The songs from its third recording, *Transfiguração*, featured more layered, acoustic textures with nylon-stringed guitars and smaller guitar-shaped instruments, such as the ten-string *viola caipira* and the ukulele-like, four-string *cavaquinho*. Live, however, the group played this softer material —including a lullaby that Lirinha wrote for his daughter—with the same volume and weight found in heavy metal and *candomblé* drumming.

At the time, however, armed with a new camera and a press pass, I stood on the side of the stage, thrilled by the intensity of the show. Between Lirinha's charismatic stage presence and the power and skill of the players, even a battleworn Cordel put on an impressive, mesmerizing show. From this new vantage point I could see what a pivotal role Jathyles, the lighting designer, played in ratcheting up the show's energy. The colors of the lighting gels and the rhythm of their changes nimbly reacted both to Lirinha's lyrics and the musical changes. Watching the video footage later, I found the strobe lights overused, but at the time they only added to the overwhelming effect of the show's menacing climaxes on the audience. The special effects featured on earlier tours—such as the police lights and the scarlet LEDs that Lirinha wore on his hands as stigmata—had broken in the in-

Figure 7.3. Ciço Gomes in street clothes, performing one more time alongside the Calixto family. *Photo by the author.*

tervening years and been left behind wherever the band happened to be playing that night, deemed too much trouble to keep repairing. Standing only a few feet from the drummers, I could see how the performance had become a job for them. There were moments when they were on autopilot. I watched them go through the motions, joking to one another with their eyebrows or thinking about what dramatic gesture to make next.

Coco Raízes, who played on the main stage after Cordel, were confronting their own personnel changes. After many years of threatening to leave and form his own group, Ciço Gomes finally left six weeks before the 2009 São João Festival so that he could rehearse with new players in time to debut the new group on one of the smaller, more peripheral stages. Fagner Gomes, the main dancer of Coco Raízes, left the group to play triangle in a *forró* band. Coco Raízes was without an improviser and MC, and the group didn't have enough time before the festival to find another, so Ciço agreed to make an appearance one last time. On the video footage that I recorded, Ciço was in rare form, weaving among the other players on the overfogged stage, bantering to the crowd, placing his hand on Assis's shoulder and singing a line to him. His jeans and striped dress shirt conspicuously contrasted with the matching lime-green floral camp shirts and floor-length dresses that the rest of the group wore (see figure 7.3). Once again, dress had indexed yet another split affecting the *samba de coco* families in Arcoverde, just as Severina Lopes's act of wearing a vest to Lula's funeral had catalyzed the splintering of the group.

With this new fissure, my efforts to remain neutral and engage with all three families once again became more difficult. I made the rounds to the Alto do Cruzeiro and down the hill to the Gomes household, but my interest in Ciço's new group made some Calixtos question my allegiances. Gomes's new group rehearsed in Ciço's house, giving me the opportunity to see a scene of *samba de coco* performed informally there that previously I had only been able to view on a 1996 videotape. Furniture was pushed against the walls of the small house, clearing a space for the musicians and dancers. Ciço was very relaxed and excited to be leading his own group, and the musicians and singers sounded good—not yet quite as tight as Coco Raízes in their interlocking rhythms and vocal harmonies, but respectable nonetheless considering that it had only been rehearsing for a month. Ciço's young grandchildren lined up and rehearsed the slower, lopsided *parcela* stomp and the quicker *trupé*, resurrecting variations of the steps that I had only seen on the 1996 videotape before Fagner and Daiane's renditions became standardized as the new original.

The group, Coco Trupé de Arcoverde, debuted on São João's Day proper on the peripheral stage far from downtown, next to the Bar da Poesia. Before Ciço went up to the stage, I asked him for permission to record video of the show, and he replied, "Of course. We are not uppity here!" (*Aqui não tem frescura!*), in a veiled reference to his former bandmates. The show was exuberant. Ciço was free to choose the songs he wanted to sing, his musicians were anxious and excited to be onstage, and no one was just going through the motions. They sang several older songs that had been banished from Coco Raízes's repertoire in favor of new songs whose authorship was uncontested. The repertoires of Coco Raízes and Coco Irmãs Lopes were effectively combined. By singing his songs and omitting the newer Calixto-penned tunes, Ciço's performance underscored how fundamental his contribution to Coco Raízes had been. A weight had been lifted off his back, and his enthusiasm was contagious. After playing their set, the band marched offstage, away from the microphones, and led the dancing crowd to the nearby Bar da Poesia. Never stopping between songs for more than a few seconds, the celebration continued inside the bar, Ciço sustaining the party by running from one group of dancers to the next and singing lines to them. I was rooting for him in his new endeavor, all the while aware that he would be starting over to a large extent in building up name recognition for performances outside of Arcoverde.

On Tour with Cordel do Fogo Encantado

Right after the São João Festival, I spent a few days traveling with Cordel on its tour bus to performances in the northeastern cities of Fortaleza and

Mossoró. After I had spent so much time dissecting the images and sounds of life on tour found in the band's video *In My Veins* (see chapter 4), it was great to experience it firsthand. I imagine my excitement, which I swallowed in an attempt to appear nonchalant and professional, was not unlike the thrill of fans coming to the Alto do Cruzeiro to stomp the *coco* with Coco Raízes. Seating on the chartered bus immediately revealed the group's divisions. Ostensibly the spatial split was an arrangement decided upon to separate the nonsmokers from the smokers, but the division appeared to run deeper than that. Emerson and certain roadies stayed way up front, while Clayton and Lirinha stayed in the back of the bus. Nego and Rafa sat in between, and the managers and support staff were interspersed throughout. Enacting a music documentary cliché, the camaraderie they projected onstage hid their offstage conflicts.

The contrast between the venues in Fortaleza, a large regional state capital, and Mossoró, a smaller city, underscored the unique and somewhat precarious position that Cordel held in the Brazilian music market, despite the critical acclaim the group had won. Cordel was not on the radar screen of young demographics that take cues from mass-market radio. Produced independently, the band relied on word of mouth within its ardent college-aged fan base. Yet there was always a flock of fans hovering around the exhausted band members after their performances. In Fortaleza they filled a large, well-equipped, and well-maintained outdoor amphitheater. In Mossoró they shared the bill with eight other bands in a disorganized festival with a more dubious infrastructure. The scaffolding above the stage was hanging so low that the swiftly rotating robotic spotlights almost bumped the musicians' heads and scorched them.

WE ALREADY TOLD THIS STORY HERE, BUT WE'RE GOING TO REPEAT IT

During each of their performances on the tour that I accompanied, there was a pivotal moment worth exploring in detail, because it bluntly condensed the cultural politics that animated the band's vision. In the middle of the song "A Matadeira (Ou no balanço da justiça)" (The slaughterhouse [or on the scales of justice]), the drummers abruptly stopped playing, and Lirinha began to speak to the crowd. The story he told and its repetition throughout the years point to the band's receding relevance at the end of the 2000s, after six years of Lula da Silva–led Brazil, in contrast to the post-dictatorship millennial moment within which it had formed. I have parsed and annotated here exactly what he proclaimed during their July 2009 performance in Fortaleza:

THE SLAUGHTERHOUSE
(OR ON THE SCALE OF JUSTICE)

Look!
The slaughterhouse is coming
To Cactus Heights/the shantytown on the hill
To scales of justice
Of your maker
The slaughterhouse is coming
To Cactus Heights/the shantytown on the hill
To scales of justice
Saltpeter gunpowder sulfur lead
The banquet of the earth
The theater of the sky
Do tell, who comes there?
The old soldier
What does he bring in his chest?
Life and death
What does he bring in his head?
The slaughterhouse
And what did he come to say?
Fire!

A MATADEIRA
(OU NO BALANÇO DA JUSTIÇA)

Vê
A matadeira vem chegando
No alto da favela
No balanço da justiça
Do seu criador
Matadeira vem chegando
No alto da favela
No balanço da justiça
Salitre pólvora enxofre chumbo
O banquete da Terra
O Teatro do céu
Diz aí quem vem lá
O velho soldado
O que traz no seu peito
A Vida e a Morte
O que traz na cabeça

A matadeira
E o que veio falar
Fogo

The song "A Matadeira" employs furious, punk-rock-like energy to decry a foundational historical event in Northeast Brazil: the 1897 massacre at Canudos, Bahia, where government troops killed thirty thousand millenarian maverick Catholics working to build a utopian society under the charismatic leadership of Antonio Conselheiro. Author and journalist Euclides da Cunha traveled from the South to chronicle the attack and eventually wrote *Os Sertões* (Rebellion in the Backlands), a historical novel about the event. *Os Sertões* is now thought to be one of the principal works in the Brazilian literary canon and an important predecessor to northeastern regionalist literature. The book contributed to the cementing of the opposition between the Northeast as a poor, violent, archaic, traditional, folkloric, mystical, rebellious space and the Southeast as a future-oriented, industrialized, modern, cosmopolitan space. It also managed to contribute to the questioning of this binary. Cordel do Fogo Encantado, therefore, had multiple investments in Canudos, as it performed popular music that engaged with the Brazilian "national question" from a regionalist position. The Canudos rebellion was crucial to the history of the region, and it spurred several decades of literature and popular culture that contributed to the shaping of the narratives of the Northeast that they seek to engage with, capitalize on, overturn, and revise.

> Fortaleza, Cordel do Fogo Encantado has already told this story here, but we're going to repeat it. Until the end of this tour, we will tell this story in all of the cities . . .

> *Fortaleza, o Cordel do Fogo Encantado já contou esta história aqui, mas vamos repetir. Até o fim dessa turné, contaremos esta história em todas as cidades . . .*

This throwaway line, recited just as the drums fell away halfway through the song, acknowledged that by the time the band was performing in a Fortaleza amphitheater in 2009, Lirinha was conscious of repeating himself. He had spent night after night running through the tightly rehearsed show and was aware that this repetition risked lessening the power of their performance.

> "The slaughterhouse" is the nickname of a German machine gun that was bought by the Brazilian government to solve a problem: to destroy a city in the backlands of the state of Bahia. This happened one hundred years ago. This city had thirty thousand inhabitants. The name of this city was . . .

> ["Canudos!" the audience yells.]

A matadeira é o apelido de uma metralhadora alemão que foi contratada pelo governo brasileiro para resolver um problema. Para destruir uma cidade no interior da Bahia. Isso aconteceu há cem anos atrás. Essa cidade tinha trinta mil habitantes. O nome dessa cidade era . . .

At this point Lirinha explained what the song was about, or as the second title in parentheses indicates, merely one of many ways to interpret the song. Musically and thematically, "A Matadeira" is also quite similar to a well-known song called "Banditismo por uma questão de classe" (Banditry as a question of class) by Cordel's peers and predecessors, Chico Science e a Nação Zumbi. It is possible to listen to the song, as I did for years before hearing Lirinha's explanation, without knowing the reference to the nickname of a particular weapon. Instead, I had always assumed that it was yet another enraged contemporary account of a violent police raid on an urban *favela* shantytown in the style of Chico Science rather than a description of a bloody, century-old massacre. In the course of the next four sentences, however, populist politics and place were mapped, and the audience was defined as a kind of political constituency.

Fortaleza, they say that no one survived. But look at us here, one hundred years later, telling this story . . .

Fortaleza, dizem que ninguém sobreviveu, mas olha a gente aqui cem anos depois, contando essa história . . .

This key statement accomplished so much. It drew a continuity between those killed at Canudos and those northeasterners present at the performance. It bound the audience to the storyteller—"look at us here," all of us speaking, listening, cheering, screaming, answering—at the same time that it situated the band's endeavor as urgent labor; Lirinha was narrating their region under siege. In the name of solidarity with those killed in Canudos, he declared the audience to be symbolic descendants of those killed at Canudos. This gesture flattened the vast social distance between the poverty-stricken members of a utopian, authoritarian, millenarian sect over one hundred years ago and a largely upper-middle-class audience of college students and intellectuals. Standing near the edge of the stage, turning to pan my camera on the crowd, I couldn't help but wonder whether the great-grandparents of selected audience members sided, at the time, with the millenarians or with the government.

Canudos was located on the Alto da *Favela*. From that point forth, the press in Rio de Janeiro began to call the constructions on the hills of Rio "*favelas*"

. . .

Canudos ficava no Alto da Favela. A partir daí, a imprensa de Rio de Janeiro começou a chamar as construções no morro do Rio de favela.

Emerson reassured me that the massacre at Canudos was a foundational historical event that nearly everyone knows about. The origin of the term *favela*, referring to the proliferation of urban hilltop shantytowns in cities such as Rio de Janeiro, São Paulo, and Recife, however, is not as well known. By recounting the etymology of the term, Lirinha worked to further one of the band's primary goals: binding together the *sertão* and the *favela* and combating representations of the two spaces as isolated, contrasting social margins within the Brazilian nation. This dialectical bringing together of the Catholic, *mestiço* cowboy culture of the *sertão* and Afro-Brazilian coastal culture often associated with the urban *favela* also animated the success and recognition of *samba de coco* in Arcoverde, the Alto do Cruzeiro serving, as I argued in chapter 4, as a *favela light* in the *sertão light*.

That time, one hundred years ago, the government ordered "the slaughter-house"; and today, has anything changed?

["No!" the audience screams.]

[Walks away from the microphone, but yells, still audibly.]

One hundred years later—has anything changed?

["No!" the audience screams even louder.]

Aquele tempo, há cem anos atrás, o governo mandou a matadeira.
E hoje—alguma coisa mudou?

[*Não!*]

Cem anos depois, e alguma coisa mudou?

[*Não!*]

This moment was pitched in the register of a populist political rally: a solemn, fiery, impassioned rally, not a *showmício*. It articulated a linkage between a past massacre and present urban police violence and expressed outrage toward it. At the same time, although the audience responded with the requisite anger and enthusiasm, that moment lingered in my mind long after the show was over. It seemed as if the question "Has anything changed?" followed by a bellowing "No!" had resonated more strongly in 1999 than it did in 2009. Granted, police response in the *favelas* has indeed been horrifying. However, over the course of the decade the apocalyptic affect deployed by Cordel had become a story already told and repeated, as group members themselves admitted on stage. Moreover, although Lirinha later stated that he believed much of the progress that Lula da Silva's Partido dos Trabalhadores (Worker's Party) had made in the area of arts and culture was more symbolic (on the level of multicultural representation) than concrete (on the level of actual redistribution of resources), the country's recent economic boom and successful antipoverty programs may make a cynical statement like "nothing has changed" resonate less strongly in a new climate.

By this point the Northeast region in particular was surging economically, posting up to double-digit growth rates. Yet as the economic boom was widely reported worldwide, the question remained to what extent this capital was reaching the majority of Brazilians. In 2013, when I returned once more, disgust over huge expenditures on the upcoming World Cup and Olympic Games spurred nationwide protests, ostensibly sparked by a 10 cent increase in bus fares. At the protests, several people could be seen angrily wearing clown noses, mirroring the title track of Cordel's second record by claiming that they were clowns in the circus without a future that they believed Brazil had become.

Repeating Yourself Is the Worst Thing an Artist Can Do

In São Paulo I met with Lirinha with a more luxurious amount of time to talk, far from the mind-fog-inducing overnight bus rides we had shared on tour in the Northeast. I brought several pages of this book in progress, which I had translated into Portuguese so that I could read and discuss them with Lirinha. I read aloud the introductory chapter outlining the contours of debates in Pernambuco at the time regarding *resgate*: cultural rescue, recovery, and revival. Lirinha responded in a way that I believe bookends the meeting of researchers that I describe at the beginning of this book. His response addresses the themes of place, heritage, memory, race, and music:

> L: The topic of *resgate*, for us, was the principal point to be argued, to be reinvented, to be thought about. Today, I think that we wasted lots of time doing this, but I only think that today. We wasted lots of time on this topic.
>
> DS: I'm returning years later, so I'm explaining what I wrote. I agree with you that the time has come to talk about other things.
>
> L: I just think it has already come and went. Lots of people understand the critique, and another group of people carry on with *resgate* and will continue. There's no way to convince them. It's a way of life. . . .
>
> At the time, it was the most important topic. And it defined, as well, the

paths that people took. You can't avoid this topic, just because its moment has passed. . . .

For me Iram's response summarizes it all: "I don't want to talk about the past." For me, that's it there . . . of course, if you were to do a deeper analysis of it, she is also afraid that she doesn't know her history.

DS: And with Damião as well, there is this, right? Because Lula Calixto knew a lot more . . .

L: Yes, Daniel, and no as well. Micheliny started her research, and for the people involved it was as much a discovery as it was for us. It's just that it's so serious to say this because the aura of the ancestors [*ancestralidade*] is in the branding of that group, isn't it? And saying that that group doesn't know, doesn't remember . . . clearly, when they start to sing, it triggers their memory—oh, I remember when my grandmother used to sing that song to lull me to sleep. Yes, the ancestral thing is there, but it is totally lost.

Resgate is a theme that has to be touched upon, I believe, because when you touch upon it, you end up branching out beyond music and Arcoverde to the entire region. What is interesting to remember about my relationship to Lula Calixto, for example? The transformation of Lula in the city, together with the restoration of his history. Putting aside Lula as a musical figure, and thinking more about the question of his humanity.

This transition from lunatic to hero, that this "lunatic" grew up black in a region with few black people that arrived to very difficult living conditions. He went along, holding tight to the shards of his history. This reminds me a lot of the [nearby indigenous group] Xukuru. It reminds me of Chicão Xukuru. He was a lot like this. He succeeded in gathering two hundred words in Xukuru. He valued these shards so much, do you understand? They lost their connecting words, but nonetheless, they figured out how to say an entire phrase. Only nouns were left.

They made a chapbook with the two hundred words. Lots of people laughed, saying that this was a lie, or that it was a linguistic error. Fuck, for me, it didn't matter. Leave this to the specialists—this kind of analytical talk that we're having right now. Leave it to the people who study linguistics and such. For me, it was a guy trying to construct his own history, you know? This is what mattered to me. Just like Lula Calixto, he remade his own history.

Remember that in Arcoverde there is just one book of historical anecdotes and reminiscing: *Minha Cidade, Minha Saudades* (My city, my nostalgia). What is shocking to me in *Minha Cidade, Minha Saudades*, is the absence. It's as if that black family didn't exist. Incredible. The author Luis Wilson is even called out as a leftist. At the time, he had problems with the large landowners and all. He was "open-minded," let's say. How could that guy frequent, according to Lula Calixto, several Coco salons? And write about Ivo Lopes, that was a *vereador* (city councilman), who tried the entire time to enter into this logic of the whites in power, so much so that he became a *vereador* for the social recognition and visibility, without mentioning that he's a great *samba de coco* singer? So, I think about this, Daniel, that much political will must have been missing, for this absence of history to have occurred. If it were an orchestra, we would probably have know[n] the founder's name, their entire career trajectory, etc.

After our interview, Lirinha played me two songs that he was working on that were emblematic of the range of genres and approaches around which he has orbited for over a decade, some associated with regional tradition, others with experimentation. The first was an imaginative cover of a Roberto Carlos song that he recorded with a producer, DJ, and electronic musician known as Buguinha. The track consisted of voice, sampled beats, and laptop-generated sequenced loops. The second was equally intriguing. It was a "duet" with venerable northeastern musician Luiz Gonzaga. Ten previously unknown instrumental Gonzaga waltzes had been uncovered, and contemporary musicians had been tapped to provide lyrics and melodies for them. The weight of the project, in which Lirinha had to sing a duet with a recording of a dead icon, had proven a burden for him. It took "forever," in his estimation, to come up with anything, because Gonzaga's presence loomed so large. The end result sounded great. His vocal inflections turned the waltz into a gritty Kurt Weill–like number. He had decided to keep the lyrics "super-simple," writing about love and missing someone in a much more straightforward way than he was used to.

Lirinha had promised his fellow bandmembers in Cordel not to release tracks like the collaboration with Buguinha, which could potentially compete with the band. As he listened to the tracks with me, however, he wavered. Maybe I should just release it, he mused. It's a great track. It's hard to resist, since I want it to be heard, he admitted. Earlier in the afternoon he had alluded to the fact that unlike Coco Raízes, which claimed that their musical caravan "hasn't died, isn't dying, nor will it die," he wanted to be upfront that Cordel's days were limited:

> L: I gave some interviews recently about the possibility of the band ending. And there are people, some of the most obnoxious guys, who reacted very badly to this possibility. And I said to them look, this rumor going around that this will be the band's last show here in Arcoverde is a lie. We plan to return for many years. Now, one day, the band is going to end. One day it'll be the end. And my big dream to complete the history of Cordel is this story of having an end. Because to dilute ourselves into a Rolling Stones–

like situation, like that, would be very sad for me, do you understand? For me, I think it'll be very important for it to end. It'll be very important for the city too. Not to have that Cordel show one day. Then the question will become: who got to see it? What kids, that will become teenagers, which ones were there? Did you see a Cordel show? Man, did you see it? Just like Lula Calixto. Did you know Lula Calixto?

DS: The interactions that you have with some of these superfans must be pretty surreal.

L: Yes. In the backlands there are some that are really into it because they feel represented for the first time. A group of a certain age. From the backlands of the *sertão*. Sertania, Tabira, São José do Egito. There are some fans that believe that Cordel is the army fighting their war, you know. A dramatization of their war. . . . It'll be important for these sentiments to be rethought someday as well. They will be rethought.

After hearing Lirinha's dream to end the band gracefully rather than enter the nostalgia circuit, their setlist frozen in time, the news eight months later that he had left the band and it had folded didn't come as much of a surprise. The seating arrangements on the tour bus—Emerson up front, Lirinha in back—had hinted at old rifts. Ultimately the democracy of the band's operations clashed with the lopsided importance of Lirinha within the band. He provided the group's lyrics, as a front man contributed to its charisma, and outlined its aesthetic and political vision. He was only one of five votes, however, and found himself consistently outvoted. Clayton, the band's guitarist, would often vote with him, but more often than not the percussionists voted as a block of three—Emerson could count on the support of Nego Enrique and Rafa. A more pragmatic, workmanlike perspective of the band as a steady job ended up steering a course that felt more and more to Lirinha like creative stagnation. Emerson's contrasting pragmatic perspective can be glimpsed in his critique of an aspect of *mangue beat* that many in Recife's "new scene" celebrated: the fact that the diverse "estuary" of *mangue beat* frowned upon other bands playing with the same instrumentation as the most successful bands in the scene, namely Chico Science and the Nação Zumbi, with their combination of Afro-Pernambucan maracatu de nação percussion and rock band instrumentation. Emerson put it this way:

We see that the result wasn't as great as it should have been, right? Because there [in Recife] the idea was to develop a new genre of music. Rock was created, rap was created, reggae was created, such-and-such genre was created, and then they created *mangue beat* there. But the thing is that they were so badly organized amongst themselves that, for example, other bands weren't allowed to work with the same format of instruments. The same as the first project of the genre, Chico Science. For example, in the punk rock scene in London, there were various bands that worked with the same crowd, practically with the same look, and that only strengthened the genre. And Recife always had the idea that every group had to be different.

The class positions of the players roughly correlate to a field of positions toward their profession. Lirinha grew up solidly middle class, his father a landowner and civil servant. He was more self-consciously intellectual and wary of getting stuck in a creative rut, conforming to the romantic notion of the charismatic, independent, and disinterested artist—what Bourdieu (1984) would define as the artistic habitus. Lirinha often found Emerson's arrangements too square and lacking in variation. Clayton and Emerson, who grew up lower middle class, were innovative with their instrumental technique, but wary of the group's experimentalism costing them fans. Their self-conception as instrumentalists tilted toward that of skilled workers or technicians. Nego Enrique and Rafa, who grew up the poorest of the group, valued keeping this well-paying and high-status job and figured that the formula shouldn't be thrown out, because it was succeeding. The creative hierarchy of the band chafed against its egalitarian governing structure. The broader tension between Cordel and Coco Raízes, marked as mutationist pop interpreter and traditionalist culture bearer, respectively, was reproduced writ small within the band's lineup. Nego Enrique and Rafa ended up falling into the role of culture bearers who brought knowledge of *candomblé* drumming, while Lirinha played the role of experimental interpreter, with Emerson and Clayton falling somewhere in between.

Memories of a Winged Coconut Frog and a Bird-Eating Tree

When I returned briefly to Arcoverde in 2013, Damião Calixto and his extended family no longer lived in the Alto do Cruzeiro. Iram's goal had been achieved: their house had been turned into a *ponto de cultura* (cultural center) funded by the national Ministry of Culture, where *samba de coco* workshops and other popular culture–themed events were hosted. It was called the Centro Cultural Mestre Assis. The space was silent now, compared to the hullaballoo of Damião's extended family. Assis was sitting out on the front step, whittling and assembling tiny wooden sandal keychain souvenirs with one of his young relatives (see figure 7.4). Styrofoam replicas of Lula Calixto's carnaval animal sculpture/costumes dangled from the ceiling in the front room. Assis invited me inside. The portrait of Lula Ca-

Figure 7.4. Assis Calixto whittles miniature wooden sandal key chains in his newly government-sponsored cultural center. *Photo by the author.*

lixto, and his hats and sandals, which were once on display in the festival mud house museum, were now hanging on the wall in the entryway of a well-equipped computer lab that occupied two of the rooms. Several professionally produced posters of the group's tours through Europe and Brazil covered the walls. All the way in the back of the house there were French doors with a small sign on them that said "Sandal-Making Workshop." But inside the small back room there weren't any sandals being made. Instead, fashioned out of painted coconut shells and wood, Assis was making whimsical and disturbing chimeras that seemed to explore his experience in the public eye "making culture" with Coco Raízes. There were a fluorescent green frog with wings and a devilish beetle with too many teeth for its mouth. The beetle had bugged-out eyes painted with "red eye," as if it were anticipating having flash pictures taken of it. A dusty coconut painted black was grinning at the viewer, its facial features attached Mr. Potato Head style. Behind it lurked a lizard-like coconut creature colored *umbanda* red and black. The creepy duo were housed inside the plastic casing of an old CRT computer monitor, as if they were an image to be viewed on the nonexistent screen (see Figure 7.5). The sculptures were hidden away. Assis wasn't selling them to visitors. He was simply letting them accumulate in the enclosed back space of his cultural center.

Back in São Paulo, Lirinha was launching his post-Cordel solo career, gig-

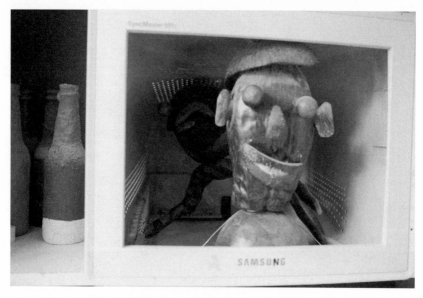

Figure 7.5. Assis Calixto's coconut-based art posed inside the shell of a computer monitor. *Photo by the author.*

ging throughout Brazil on a recently finished recording that he offered as a legal free download online. One track, "Memória" (Memory), is a peppy, unabashedly pop number that contrasts starkly with the brooding sounds of Cordel. Although it is neither *brega*, nor as flashy as *forró estilizado*, it would fit much better alongside those "barbeque restaurant"–style sounds in a DJ's playlist than Cordel would. The bubblegum pop sound, peppered throughout with Lirinha's malicious, sarcastic sung laugh, distances him from Cordel as he essentially asks—"Do you remember? Way back when? Back when I used to replant your memories of what the São João harvest festival and your region signified?"—even though it had only been three years since the band dissolved. He ended the song with a line that outlines how he viewed the movement of sounds from marginal to traditional under the genre category of *música de raíz* (roots music): "My story is a song of drunks made into a tree that eats birds," which I would paraphrase as "The story of *samba de coco* in Arcoverde is one in which a drunken recreational musical pastime was transformed into folklore and patrimony, with its implied arboreal rootedness and genealogies of cultural transmission. Cordel then took that tree and worked to strip it of its harmlessness and make it predatory again, so that it would more resemble a winged raptor than a rooted tree."

MEMORY

Do you remember?
It was the harvest festival
Do you remember?
Some soldiers that danced
I know about the cerebral circuit that recollects
The construction of what happened in the frontal lobe
But I returned to replant your memory

Inside the archives of the past
The ability to remember another time
of the future wind that blew through the flower of time
that will cause a chemical change
I go against the grain of your memory

My story is a song of drunks
Made into a tree that eats birds

MEMÓRIA

Lembra?
Era festa da colheita
Lembra?
Uns soldados que dançavam
Sei do circuito cerebral da recordação
A construção do que passou no lobo frontal
Mas eu voltei pra replantar a tua memória

Dentro dos arquivos do passado
Capacidade de lembrar em outro tempo
do vento futuro que passou na flor do tempo
Vai alteração química vou no contratempo
da tua memória

A minha história é canção de bêbados
Feito uma árvore que come pássaros

Epilogue

The *trupé*, a dance to tamp down a dirt floor, accomplishes practical labor as it celebrates it. It is an idealized image of the joyous collective construction of a home. Sophisticated, nimble samba stepping won't do—this job requires a heavier stomp that, when performed by many dancers at once, sounds like a freight train thundering past. The ground beneath the dancers is malleable, and the stomping is an artistic practice that through physical exertion makes a tangible impact on a place upon which the dancers have staked claim. The dance step, with its ability to leave an imprint that changes the terrain, serves as an apt gesture representing musicians' ventures "making culture" in the public sphere.

The projection of this story, this sound, and this bodily action of making culture has unfolded in a particular place and at a particular time. But as specific as the Arcoverde case is, it is a story that allows us to listen more broadly to a postauthoritarian moment. It chronicles how redemocratization and the expansion of citizenship coexist in tension with neoliberal efforts to profit from tourist destinations.

Performances such as *samba de coco*'s *trupé*, pitched and received in a nostalgic register, have entered nesting local, regional, and national networks of public and private sponsorship. Arcoverde's musicians navigate the often-conflicting visions of several overlapping institutions, entering an arena where, using Holston's (2008) language, insurgent and entrenched notions of cultural citizenship are currently being worked on. During the years that Coco Raízes and Cordel formed and flourished, the MST encampments and the *favela* shantytowns thrust rural and urban struggles over land and shelter into the national spotlight.

Expressions of older entrenched citizenship, with its inclusive rhetoric papering over a grossly lopsided distribution of rights, can be found in the impulse to visit Arcoverde as a kind of *favela light*. To such visitors, *samba de coco* features an idealized performance of autoconstruction without menace or complication, a welcome escape for certain middle-class Recifenses reluctantly caught in the intensifying fortification of high-rise living in the state capital. The nostalgia animating the sojourn can be seen as an attempt to locate a place where the easy mixture of races and social classes found within the story of samba can still be found (Carvalho 2004).

But whether or not this type of nostalgia underlies some of the visitors' expectations, it is not the only way to interpret the significance of these performances of Arcoverde. The diverging artistic trajectories of Coco Raízes and Cordel can be better understood, I believe, as strategies of positioning vis-à-vis insurgent challenges to entrenched citizenship and its links to the aging but durable samba and MPB paradigms. While some visitors see Arcoverde as an escape back to older notions of cordial social mixture, Coco Raízes can also be seen as reworking the São João script within a newer notion of multiculturalism, an assertion of Afro-Brazilian-ness in *mestiço* cowboy country. And Cordel works to make sanitized folkloric tropes dangerous again by drawing upon and overturning both nostalgic and apocalyptic literary and cinematic images of their region as a territory of poverty.

Whether operating within an alternative, mutationist genre or as traditionalist roots music with a heavy emphasis on the musicians' role as culture bearers, both groups use restorative and reflective nostalgia to occupy a field in which these new ideas of citizenship are coming to the fore. The extended temporalities of the popular music of Cordel and Coco Raízes revisit as far back as the late nineteenth-century beginnings of the republic, pointing to a return to reassess the Brazilian national question during a moment of postdictatorship cultural reckoning.

Several marks of this postauthoritarian moment can be found within the Arcoverde case. In the 1990s and 2000s Lirinha attempted to temper the reassuring sentimentality of much of the era's cinematic rediscovery of deep, authentic Brazil through his engagement with radical 1960s film theories such as the aesthetics of hunger. The presence in Arcoverde of Dona Amélia, the representative of the state arts funding agency Fundarpe who helped bring together the *samba de coco* families, was the result of decentralization efforts that sent officials throughout the state. Public support for such a markedly Afro-Brazilian assertion of difference in the interior fit within a new multicultural politics of difference interacting with older discourses of cultural and racial mixture.

The postauthorization moment is also characterized by the expansion and policing of intellectual property rights and anxieties over digital copying. In Brazil piracy has been emerging as central, and efforts to "apply IP to as broad a range of human practices as possible" (Dent 2012, 44) characterized the 2000s. This was understood by Arcoverde's musical families as a threat to their efforts to move from the margins to the center.

For *samba de coco* musicians, the goal of having their recordings circulate in the formal economic sector, rather than having only pirated copies circulating informally, has become a marker of their newly recognized cultural citizenship. And during the 1990s and 2000s, when the musical commodity was transforming irrevocably from LP to CD to digitally circulating MP3, its tangibility as a material object vanishing, musicians worked to anchor themselves to a destination by gathering artifacts. This building of museums shored up the families' claims to repertoires of nebulous authorship (in strict legal terms) as they professionalized.

The musicians assert themselves not only through their songs, but also through this extramusical building up of the materiality of place. The São João Festival featured an official exhibit of a mud house museum that displayed Lula Calixto's and Ivo Lopes's personal effects. The Calixto and Lopes families in turn decided to build their own exhibits telling their own stories and planned to build a tourist destination with a mud house of their own. They worked with their sponsors to secure a voice in the public sphere and worked independently to build up their own enterprises as well. They welcomed long-term ethnographers and invited visitors, treating them as weekend-long ethnographers.

Fundarpe, the SESC, municipal support of tourism, and Rec-Beat all follow different recipes of sponsorship, their ratios of traditionalist and mutationist acts varying with their mission statements. Fundarpe is more traditionalist and commerce averse; Rec-Beat is more mutationist, contemporary, and commercial. The municipality has a stake in putting the city on the map and turning the locality into a destination for commerce and visitors. The SESC sponsors a variety of events, and its criteria seem to be more tied to an assessment of cultural substance and, more often than not, an engagement with Brazilian-ness, rather than to a strict traditionalist/mutationist split. In certain venues place-specific mutationist acts substitute for older notions of traditionalism. Focusing on both traditionalism and Brazil-specific mutationism allows these institutions to engage with the contemporary while passing over acts that don't feature a certain quotient of musical Brazilian-ness, such as foreign and Brazilian acts working firmly within US genres of pop, rock, and hip-hop. Traditionalism and place-based mutationism work in tandem to effectively promote festival destinations that cater to various demographics while remaining tied to a sense of locality. Reassuring restorative nostalgia and bittersweet, reflective nostalgia are mutually sustaining to fans who savor groups that perform genre liquidity and also groups that perform genre fixity. Through the circulatory flows of fans seeking the sources of the mixes they love, each mode nourishes the other.

Yet there is an uneasiness to this arrangement that persists in the ways in which traditionalist groups are received across the oral/literate divide. The literate call the illiterate and semiliterate *Mestre*, marvel at their skills of oral dexterity and improvisation, and stand in awe of the speed of their dance steps. The educated become the students, and those with less formal education are placed in the role of teacher. What is downplayed in these dramatized reversals of power relations is that the illiterate and semiliterate in places like Arcoverde lack reading skills not because they occupy a position that is radically outside of Brazilian modernity, but because they occupy a lower rung in a stratified system of social class that denies them educational opportunities. Lula Calixto, as a child, did not understand how injections prevented or treated illness, not because vaccinations were a deeply foreign cultural practice, but simply because he did not have regular access to the clinic a few kilometers up the road. With this reversal, poverty (a fate the poor do not generally wish upon themselves) is celebrated as a virtue.

At the end of his career Mário de Andrade acknowledged that this reversal of who is considered the authority and who is considered the apprentice, so often celebrated within folklore, was predicated on a chasm between social classes. This concerned him because he was committed to narrowing this chasm in the name of social justice. The shifts in notions of folklore and heritage detailed in this book can be productively seen in this light, I believe. Neither the rescued nor the rescuer feels comfortable in his or her role in this drama, and both are reaching beyond this older script and into new territory. And through their strides to democratize control over performance spaces, they are achieving many of their goals.

The Calixtos' bar and cultural space is one such opened space, and their entrepreneurial dreams for their own tourist infrastructure are grander still. As Coco Raízes tour and perform, recognition elsewhere increases their local clout, affording them more leverage in negotiating with the municipal government and controlling the terms of their sponsorship. Coco Raízes have made considerable inroads into the circuits of the music industry, where many other marginal-turned-traditional groups gain access only to the stage covered in palm fronds. The Lopes sisters, for example, have worked tirelessly to revive their family's flagging status as an emblem of Arcoverde's popular culture. Although they do not have access to some of the performance opportunities outside of Pernambuco that Coco Raízes do, they have succeeded locally in maintaining government support. Coco Raízes have succeeded, in part, by following through on connections made through Cordel. They are frank about how Cordel helps promote them when they sing the lyric, "Cordel Encantado is our great friend. It's life, it's culture, it's helping us get the word out." The Calixto family have even cre-

Figure E.1. Assis Calixto entertains his neighbor as he rides "Bob's Goat."
Photo by the author.

ated their own fantastical chimera to represent themselves: a taxidermied goat with a dreadlocked wig on a skateboard called the *Bode do Bob* (Bob's Goat), in homage to the reggae singer Bob Marley (see figure E.1).

At the same time, the reception of the *Bode do Bob* offers an example of how, within this complex field of cultural production, attempts by musicians marked as traditionalist to venture into mutationist territory can leave them vulnerable to deflating their own appeal. There is pressure on traditionalists to play their scripted role. During the filming of the Globo network television documentary, the camera operators took pains to avoid placing the dreadlocked goat on a skateboard within their field of view. Perhaps monstrous and nonsensical on first glance, the *Bode do Bob*, prominently placed in the Calixtos' self-run museum, can be seen as a cosmopolitan self-representation. In this way, it parallels the logo of Recife's *mangue beat*—a satellite dish sitting in the mangrove swamp mud—about which so much has been written in discussing Brazilian popular music and globalization. *Mangue beat*'s logo juxtaposes a local emblem (the mangrove swamp) with an emblem of the global (an instant media feed from the rest of the world), using an object of contemporary consumer culture (a satellite dish) to communicate the local/global and folk/pop tensions underlying the music scene. Similarly, The *Bode do Bob* combines a regional emblem (a goat) with a global pop icon (Bob Marley), nailing it down to an object of contemporary consumer culture (a skateboard).

The grotesque Rastafarian goat on wheels disrupts the sanctity of taxidermic naturalism by foregrounding artifice. The Globo TV network camera operators' avoidance of Bob's Goat can be seen as an attempt to counter this disruption and to restore the innocent register of quaint folkloric tradition. In order for nostalgic traditions that signal the past to be reassuring rather than haunting, the uncanny must be reined in, as it "lies in some uncertainty about what is real or imaginary, self or other" in terrain that is both familiar and unfamiliar, home and not home (Ivy 1995, 84). Navigating this in-between-ness effectively means the difference between the harmless rag doll heralding a celebration of Arcoverde's mythical past and the monstrous goat chimera from which visitors avert their eyes. It is the difference between the folkloric first phase of Cordel's theatrical spectacle, in which the call to ancestors was accompanied by a soothing, consonant progression on guitar, and the subsequent phases of the group, in which the exact same words were accompanied by an ominous, cinematic soundtrack that echoed the classic film *Frankenstein*.

Moving between the nostalgic register of folklore and a harsher heavy metal–influenced apocalyptic register of gothic horror was one of the means by which Cordel struggled to transcend the self-described prison of being labeled a folklore-based northeastern regional group. Its particular brand of "refurbished folklorism" (Ivy 1995, 60) gestured toward danger and flirted with it before returning to safer terrain. Take the trademark use of the *candeeiro* lantern: the flickering of the flames next to Lirinha's face can be seen as either a quaint invocation of a past before electricity, or as lighting that is spooky and disquieting. Like a clown in a threadbare circus on the dangerous outskirts of town, the band was by turns threatening and ebullient in its performances. On stage the group occupied a universe in which contemporary lived Arcoverde and the literary and cinematic backlands intermingled. Incorporating *sertão*-associated rhythms with Afro-Brazilian religious drumming associated with urban *favelas,* Cordel melded together the rural and the urban. Incorporating traditional music with an aggressive heavy metal sensibility, it pitted nostalgia against a pointedly antinostalgic temporality set in an apocalyptic end-time that is all eschaton and no origin. By incorporating Brechtian distancing techniques and a measured amount of Artaud's "Theatre of Cruelty," the group sought to defamiliarize this nostalgic folklorism that normally acts to reassure.

Cordel's use of techniques from radical avant-garde drama served both to distance them from traditionalism and to add to the band's symbolic capital by positioning it as a pop band operating in an intellectual register. The same can be said of its constant ventriloquism of folk and canonic literary poets, which served as key references invoking past intellectual treatments of the question of Brazilian identity. As Stewart and Shaw suggest, a new brand of authenticity foregrounding the hybrid counters traditionalist purism by inverting it, but it too risks becoming an "unreflective badge of sophistication" (1994, 22–23) used for the purposes of social distinction (Bourdieu 1984). The band members talked about the elite status of their market niche almost as a necessary evil on their path to national recognition. In an interview Clayton stated, "[We] constantly strive to make our work less elite, to not let ourselves be influenced by people from high society, or by people who are intelligent, in quotation marks," aware of the challenges of working as a northeastern artist in São Paulo. Cordel was keenly aware of its audience, and although much of the curious local crowd at the free São João performance in Arcoverde stood baffled and in awe, the band's ventures into gothic horror ultimately stopped short of alienating the paying crowds.

Cordel's decision to dramatize contact with *samba de coco* and *reisado* in Arcoverde as it performed outside the region has had many consequences. By tying itself to a mappable point of origin, it inspired fans to travel there in hopes of having their own contact experiences, like those about which the band had sung so passionately. This led to an ethnographic fieldwork-like experience as heritage tourism, contributing to the social and commercial recognition of the group's musical mentors Coco Raízes, the unwelcome pressure for Coco Raízes to stay in Arcoverde, and the drive to build their own site of origins in Rio da Barra. In recent decades the disenfranchised majority have altered the Brazilian terrain by insisting on asserting their economic and political rights. Yet despite the heartening progress of "insurgent citizenship," the notion still persists that only the few are to be treated as full citizens. In large Brazilian cities like Recife, the growth of *favela* shantytowns and fortified high-rises side by side manifests the friction that exists between these zones that harbor conflicting ideas of citizenship. In Arcoverde *samba de coco* and Cordel, taken together, offer a case study of how a canonized periphery just far enough from the culturally dominant coast served not as an escape from this friction, but as a unique site where what it means to be Brazilian was being worked upon.

Notes

Introduction

1. The Pernambuco *sertão* stands just beyond the reach of the principal colonial economic cycles (such as brazil wood, sugarcane, tobacco, and coffee) that influenced the geographical distribution of significant numbers of Afro-Brazilians (Araújo dos Anjos 2011, 265). While coastal areas around cities such as Recife, Pernambuco, and Salvador, Bahia, that were active in the slave trade have large Afro-Brazilian populations to this day, the northeastern interior is characterized as more strongly influenced by indigenous and Luso-Brazilian cultural flows. That said, Arcoverde is in the same vicinity as the seventeenth-century fugitive community of escaped slaves and others—the *Quilombo dos Palmares*—located only 180 kilometers away. So while Afro-Brazilians may be less culturally prominent in Arcoverde, the broader region is strongly associated with a history of Afro-Brazilian resistance.

2. The Cordel referred to here is a folklore revue turned musical group, not to be confused with *literatura de cordel,* pamphlets of folk poetry traditionally sold hanging from twine at open air markets.

3. For a discussion of the para-ethnographic, see Ong and Collier (2005, 235–252).

1. Staging Tradition

1. Taussig terms this impulse to view the response of people from the hinterlands upon seeing new inventions a "frontier ritual of technological superiority" (1993, 208).

2. The SESC's activities are defined within the areas of education, health, leisure, culture, and medical assistance.

3. The harmonies, male and female, consisted of parallel thirds and sixths. All of the songs were in major keys, although the seventh scale degree was sometimes flatted, as is common in *sertão* styles such as *forró* and *cantoria de viola*. Also in contrast to many Afro-diasporic musics that use asymmetrical rhythmic timelines, *samba de coco* vocal melodies stress the same beats that the percussion stresses (the one beat and the and-of-two), rather than accenting gaps in the percussion parts and emphasizing a polyrhythmic feel. Melodies are dextrously delivered on few

pitches, often hanging on a single pitch for several consecutive eighth notes. It made sense that *mangue beat* pioneer Chico Science fused *coco* and hip-hop, because the staccato vocal acrobatics of the two genres are compatible, although *coco* melodies are more rhythmically fixed and regular than hip-hop vocals, and unlike most hip-hop, they aren't swung.

4. Ariano Suassuna is an important figure in the Pernambucan cultural landscape. As a playwright and a novelist, he spearheaded the Movimento Armorial, which was dedicated to the creation of an erudite art that highlighted connections between northeastern folklore and forms of music and art from the baroque period. As secretary of culture he was influential in shaping Pernambucan traditionalism.

5. R and L stand for right and left feet. Accented steps are represented by bold uppercase letters. Periods represent ghosted steps that are almost inaudible.

6. The soaring vocal melody traveled up from the tonic and hit a note somewhere between a major and a minor third in the Western tempered scale. The scale, exotic for most of Brazil, as well as the singer's ornamented style, placed it far into the desertlike *sertão* of the Northeastern region. *Aboio*'s superficial musical affinity with the Arab muslim call to prayer gave the *aboio* vocalizations a magnetism that pulled toward invoking another place and/or another time period.

7. While the accompaniment in the first version follows a circle of fifths in a major key, the accompaniment of the second version begins on C, leaps up a tritone, and then slithers down back to the C, the dominant of F phrygian, without resolving. The repeating melody creeps along in truncated, irregular 15/8 time. It appears to occupy the clichéd function that Bach's Toccata and Fugue in D Minor has come to perform in horror movies with scenes set in haunted houses.

2. Museums

1. When the Lopes, Calixto, and Gomes families first began to play together, the group was called A Caravana de Ivo Lopes, in homage to the prominent *coco* musician performing in the city from the 1950s through the 1970s.

2. At the time the federal government had recently begun a program of awarding special funding to *remanescentes de quilombo*—communities that could be historically tied to these escaped slave communities, not unlike programs exclusively for indigenous communities administered by Brazil's department focusing on indigenous affairs, FUNAI.

3. The *berimbau* is a kind of musical bow most often played to accompany the Afro-Brazilian dance/game/martial art capoeira.

4. This phrase, translated as "making" or "doing culture," was first brought to my attention by ethnomusicologist Cristina Barbosa.

3. Nostalgia and Apocalypse

1. Os Gêmeos ("twins" in Portuguese) are identical twin graffiti artists Otavio and Gustavo Pandolfo from São Paulo. The twins have received official recogni-

tion in the art world since this description from 2004, including a featured role in the 2008 Tate Modern exhibition *Street Art in London*.

2. Susan Stewart's comment about the transformation from country music to bluegrass resonates here. She describes country music as "played at the speed of the audience" at rest, as opposed to bluegrass music, which "mimes the movements of the machine that reproduces it," pitting "the limits of skill against the limits of aural speed." For all its nods to tradition, she finds this acceleration "a testament to technology; its referent is the history of mechanical innovation and not simply the history of musical innovation" (Stewart 1993, 12).

3. As I explore Cordel's genre shifts, I rely on Dent's framework for understanding the mutual constitution of "traditionalist" and "mutationist" genres (2012, 102). Dent remains aware of the ways in which "actors, institutions and practices explicitly and implicitly use genre for a variety of tasks" (92) that affect how and where music is received. From record store bin categories (which still mattered when these groups began) to the expectations of critics and concert-goers, genres remain a moving target with concrete consequences for musicians' access to particular venues and media outlets. Yet even as genre steers how a musical work is interpreted, its power to shape expectations is often underacknowledged.

4. Micheliny Verunschk, "*Transfiguração*: um roteiro de leitura" (unpublished manuscript, July 13, 2009).

5. Track 19 of Cordel do Fogo Encantado's self-titled first CD (Rec-Beat 2001).

4. Television

1. The Globo television network, which produced the *Globo Comunidade* program on *samba de coco*, is a powerful producer of representations of Brazilian-ness disseminated throughout the nation and beyond. Straubhaar provides a good entrance into the extensive literature on Brazilian media and specifically the Globo network (Straubhaar 1989, 140–154) He characterizes Globo as "a major element of the Brazilian power structure" (148) due to its extensive vertical and horizontal integration of the media marketplace, including control over "radio, music recording, newspapers, and publishing, as well as industries outside the media such as fashion and real estate" (142) in the 1990s, and this market domination continues into the present. The network "dominates the audience and ratings thoroughly, capturing 60 to 80 percent of the audience most of the time" (141) and more than 60 percent of advertising revenue. Straubhaar argues that the economic power of the Globo network, which essentially rose with the 1964 military dictatorship (141), is such that the state has less mediating power in its programming than most corporatist states. That said, currently there is a heterogeneity of representations of popular culture on the network. My analysis here focuses only on *Globo Comunidade*, a Sunday morning program that frequently produces segments on popular culture pitched in a register of rescue and recovery.

2. Almeida (2004).

3. Florianópolis is the capital city of the southern Brazilian state Santa Catarina.

4. *Samba de Coco Raízes de Arcoverde* (2003), track 2.

5. The saying is derived from Coca Light, the Brazilian name for Diet Coke.

5. Festival

1. *Forró estilizado* or "stylized *forró*" is an ultrapopular style of *forró*: accordion-based dance music associated with the northeastern *sertão* but consumed throughout Brazil. *Forró estilizado* is performed in glitzy pop productions with drumset, horns, electronic keyboards, and large groups of background dancers, as opposed to *forró pé-de-serra*, a style with the ensemble of *zabumba* bass drum, triangle, and accordion standardized by Luiz Gonzaga.

2. *Pastoril* is a folkloric dramatic dance performed during the Christmas season, in which dancers and musicians wear brightly colored costumes.

3. See the 1977 film *O palhaço degolado* (The beheaded clown) by experimental filmmaker and member of the late 1960s *Pernambucália* scene Jomard Muniz de Brito for a precedent for Lirinha's figure of the enraged clown. The footage for the short was filmed in Super 8 during the dictatorship in a prison that has since been turned into a Casa de Cultura, each cell a small boutique selling artisanal wares.

4. Perrone (1989, 24–29) and Béhague (1980, 444–447) include in-depth analyses of the Construção.

6. Tourism

1. Equating civilization with repression and seeing racialized others as somehow "id-like" and therefore less repressed is a common countercultural projection, the consequences of which are critically analyzed by Monson (1995).

2. Mestre Ambrósio, "Pé-de-calçada" (1999).

3. Green, at least, at that time in that particular year. Although Arcoverde receives more rain than many parts of the nearby *sertão*, it too depends for its greenery on a fluctuating amount of rainfall.

4. *Alastrado*, also known as *xique-xique*, is a ubiquitous shrubby cactus found throughout the Brazilian *sertão*.

5. Celpe is the state-owned utility that provides electricity. The acronym stands for A Companhia de Eletricidade de Pernambuco (the Pernambucan Electrical Company).

6. *Nu Brazil 2*, released on the label Union Square Music, and *Brazilounge*, released on Difference Music.

7. Rose Mary's brother-in-law Jonas would certainly take issue with Potter's claim to have "brought the first jazz group to arcoverde," as Jonas was one of the original saxophonists in the touring big band Super OARA, the Orquestra Arcoverdense de Ritmos Americanos (Arcoverdian Orchestra of American Rhythms), which has been playing jazz all over Brazil for four decades. But debunking Potter's claim, which was made casually after a brief visit, is not my objective.

Rather, what is more interesting is how his story of a journey to the margins to be reinvigorated by the "very powerful stuff" found in oral musical traditions is a variation on an old and often-told script.

8. It is interesting to note that both places—Pernambuco and New Orleans— are privileged in terms of their abstract or allegorical inclusion within their respective nations, while concrete social exclusion remains durable, as the aftermath of Hurricane Katrina, in the New Orleans case, has made unavoidably clear.

9. Biu Neguinho's samba school performed urban *samba de enredo* in Arcoverde in the style of Rio de Janeiro's Carnaval during the 1960s and 1970s. Damião Calixto played *pandeiro* in the group.

10. There is an extensive literature on the politics of collaboration between Western pop musicians and musicians from poorer parts of the African diaspora. Projects spearheaded by Paul Simon, David Byrne, Peter Gabriel, and Ry Cooder are the most well-known and lucrative examples and as such have been most closely scrutinized by ethnomusicologists. Meintjes (1990), Keil and Feld (1994, 238–246), and Erlmann (1996) examine the intertwined issues of cultural politics, ownership, and musical style in Paul Simon's *Graceland* record. Both Ry Cooder's relationship with Buena Vista Social Club and Potter's relationship with Coco Raízes are international collaborations in which the US musician does not have firm control over the narrative marketed and consumed, and the musicians being "discovered" end up centrally located as protagonists in the story.

11. Cordel do Fogo Encantado (2000), track 6.

12. Albuquerque Jr. (1999); Vianna and Chasteen (1999).

Bibliography

Albuquerque, Durval Muniz de, Jr. 1999. *A invencao do Nordeste e outras artes*. Serie Estudos e Pesquisas. São Paulo: Cortez Editora.

Almeida, Karla (Producer/Reporter). 2004. *Globo Comunidade*, June 18. Rio de Janeiro: TV Globo.

Andrade, Mário de. 1959. *Danças dramáticas do Brasil*. São Paulo: Martins.

Araújo dos Anjos, Rafael S. 2011. "Cartografia da Diáspora África—Brasil." *Revista da ANPEGE* 7 (1): 261–274.

Avelar, Idelber, and Christopher Dunn. 2011. *Brazilian Popular Music and Citizenship*. Durham, N.C.: Duke University Press.

Béhague, Gerard. 1980. "Brazilian Musical Values of the 1960s and 1970s: Popular Urban Music from Bossa Nova to Tropicalia." *Journal of Popular Culture* 14 (3): 437–452.

Bourdieu, Pierre. 1984. *Distinction: A Social Critique of the Judgement of Taste*. Cambridge, Mass.: Harvard University Press.

Boym, Svetlana. 2001. *The Future of Nostalgia*. New York: Basic Books.

Bredekamp, Horst. 1995. *The Lure of Antiquity and the Cult of the Machine: The Kunstkammer and the Evolution of Nature, Art, and Technology*. Princeton, N.J.: M. Wiener Publishers.

Briggs, Charles L., and Richard Bauman. 1992. "Genre, Intertextuality, and Social Power." *Journal of Linguistic Anthropology* 2 (2): 131–172.

Brustein, Robert Sanford. 1964. *The Theatre of Revolt: An Approach to the Modern Drama*. Boston: Little, Brown.

Cabral de Melo Neto, João. 1994. *João Cabral de Melo Neto – Obras Completas*. Rio de Janeiro: Editora Nova Aguilar S.A.

Carvalho, José Jorge. 2004. *Metamorfoses das tradições performáticas Afro-Brasileiras: de patrimonio cultural a indústria de entretenimento*. Série Antropologia 354. Brasília: Universidade de Brasília.

Cascudo, Luís da Câmara. 2004. *Vaqueiros e cantadores*. São Paulo: Global Editora.

Clifford, James. 1997. *Routes: Travel and Translation in the Late Twentieth Century*. Cambridge, Mass.: Harvard University Press.

Clifford, James, and George E. Marcus. 1986. *Writing Culture: The Poetics and Politics of Ethnography*. Berkeley: University of California Press.

Cunha, Euclides da. *Os sertões: campanha de Canudos*. São Paulo: Ateliê Editorial, Imprensa Oficial do Estado, Arquivo do Estado, 2001.

Dent, Alexander S. 2012. "Piracy, Circulatory Legitimacy, and Neoliberal Subjectivity in Brazil." *Cultural Anthropology* 27 (1): 28–49.

Erlmann, Veit. 1996. *Nightsong: Performance, Power, and Practice in South Africa*. Chicago: University of Chicago Press.

Feld, Steven. 1996. "Pygmy POP: A Genealogy of Schizophonic Mimesis." *Yearbook for Traditional Music* 28 (January 1): 1–35.

Flores, William Vincent, and Rina Benmayor. 1997. *Latino Cultural Citizenship: Claiming Identity, Space, and Rights*. Boston: Beacon Press.

Galinsky, Philip. 2002. *"Maracatu atômico": Tradition, Modernity, and Postmodernity in the Mangue Movement of Recife, Brazil*. New York: Routledge.

Gasperin, E. 2000. "Nacao de todos os sons: O projeto musica do Brasil." *SHOWBiZZ* i5 (2): 28–35.

Gautier, Ana María Ochoa. 2006. "Sonic Transculturation, Epistemologies of Purification and the Aural Public Sphere in Latin America." *Social Identities* 12 (6): 803–825.

Holston, James. 2008. *Insurgent Citizenship: Disjunctions of Democracy and Modernity in Brazil*. Princeton, N.J.: Princeton University Press.

Hood, Mantle. 1971. *The Ethnomusicologist*. New York: McGraw-Hill.

Ivy, Marilyn. 1995. *Discourses of the Vanishing: Modernity, Phantasm, Japan*. Chicago: University of Chicago Press.

Keil, Charles, and Steven Feld. 1994. *Music Grooves: Essays and Dialogues*. Chicago: University of Chicago Press.

Kirshenblatt-Gimblett, Barbara. 1998. *Destination Culture: Tourism, Museums, and Heritage*. Berkeley: University of California Press.

——. 2004. "Intangible Heritage as Metacultural Production." *Museum International* 56 (1–2): 52–65.

Kubik, Gerhard. 1979. *Angolan Traits in Black Music, Games and Dances of Brazil: A Study of African Cultural Extensions Overseas*. Lisboa: Junta de Investigações Científicas do Ultramar.

MacCannell, Dean. 1999. *The Tourist: A New Theory of the Leisure Class*. Berkeley: University of California Press.

Marques, Ana Claudia. 2002. *Intrigas e questões: Vingança de família e tramas sociais no sertão de Pernambuco*. Rio de Janeiro: Relume Dumará, Núcleo de Antropologia da Política.

Matta, Roberto da. 1993. *Conta de mentiroso: Sete ensaios de antropologia brasileira*. Rio de Janeiro: Rocco.

Meintjes, Louise. 1990. "Paul Simon's Graceland, South Africa, and the Mediation of Musical Meaning." *Ethnomusicology* 34 (1): 37–73.

Monson, Ingrid. 1995. "The Problem with White Hipness: Race, Gender and Cultural Conceptions in Jazz Historical Discourse." *Journal of the American Musicological Society* 48 (3): 396–422.

Nagib, Lúcia. 2003. *The New Brazilian Cinema*. London; New York: Palgrave Macmillan.

Ong, Aihwa, and Stephen J. Collier. 2005. *Global Assemblages: Technology, Politics, and Ethics as Anthropological Problems*. Malden, Mass.: Blackwell Publishing.

Perrone, Charles A. 1989. *Masters of Contemporary Brazilian Song: MPB, 1965–1985*. Austin: University of Texas Press.

Perrone, Charles A., and Christopher Dunn. 2001. *Brazilian Popular Music & Globalization*. Gainesville: University Press of Florida.

Rabinow, Paul, George E. Marcus, James D. Faubion, and Tobias Rees. 2008. *Designs for an Anthropology of the Contemporary*. Durham, N.C.: Duke University Press.

Reily, Suzel Ana. 2002. *Voices of the Magi: Enchanted Journeys in Southeast Brazil*. Chicago: University of Chicago Press.

Rony, Fatimah Tobing. 1996. *The Third Eye: Race, Cinema, and Ethnographic Spectacle*. Durham, N.C.: Duke University Press.

Sharp, Daniel Benson. 2001. "A Satellite Dish in the Shantytown Swamps: Musical Hybridity in the 'New Scene' of Recife, Pernambuco, Brazil." Master's thesis, University of Texas, Austin.

Stewart, Charles, and Rosalind Shaw. 1994. *Syncretism/Anti-syncretism: The Politics of Religious Synthesis*. London; New York: Routledge.

Stewart, Susan. 1993. *On Longing: Narratives of the Miniature, the Gigantic, the Souvenir, the Collection*. Durham, N.C.: Duke University Press.

Stokes, Martin. 2004. "Music and the Global Order." *Annual Review of Anthropology* 33: 47–72.

Straubhaar, Joseph D. 1989. "Television and Video in the Transition from Military to Civilian Rule in Brazil." *Latin American Research Review* 24 (1) 140–154.

Taussig, Michael T. 1993. *Mimesis and Alterity: A Particular History of the Senses*. New York: Routledge.

Teles, José. 1998. *Meteoro Chico*. Recife: Editora Bagaço.

———. 2000. *Do frevo ao manguebeat*. São Paulo: Editora 34.

Vianna, Hermano, and John Charles Chasteen. 1999. *The Mystery of Samba: Popular Music & National Identity in Brazil*. Chapel Hill: University of North Carolina Press.

Xavier, Ismail. 1997. *Allegories of Underdevelopment: Aesthetics and Politics in Modern Brazilian Cinema*. Minneapolis: University of Minnesota Press.

Yúdice, George. 2003. *The Expediency of Culture: Uses of Culture in the Global Era*. Durham, N.C.: Duke University Press.

Discography

Brazilounge 3: New Electro-World Rhythms from Brazil. 2004. Lisbon: EMI Different World.

Cordel do Fogo Encantado. 2001. *Cordel do Fogo Encantado*. Recife: Rec-Beat.

———. 2002. *O palhaço do circo sem futuro*. Recife: Rec-Beat.

———. 2006. *Transfiguração*. Recife: Rec-Beat.

Mestre Ambrósio. 1999. *Fuá na casa do Cabral*. Manaus, Brasil: Sony BMG Music Entertainment: Chaos.

Nu Brazil 2. 2004. Cowley, UK: Union Square Music.

Recife: Associação Educação Meio do Mundo. 2005. Recife: UFPE; João Pessoa: UFPB.

Responde a roda outra vez: Musica tradicional de Pernambuco e da Paraíba no Trajeto da Missão de 1938. 2004. Recife: Associação Respeita Januário.

Samba de Coco Raízes de Arcoverde. 2001. *Raízes de Arcoverde.* Recife: Africa Produções.

———. 2003. *Samba de coco raízes de Arcoverde.* Recife: Via Som.

Tiné. 2004. *Segura o Cordão.* Independently released.

Filmography

Diegues, Carlos
   2003—*Deus é Brasileiro (God is Brazilian)*
Ferreira, Lírio
   2006—Árido Movie *(Arid Movie)*
Rocha, Glauber
   1964—*Deus e o Diabo na Terra do Sol (Black God, White Devil)*
   1967—*Terra em Transe (Entranced Earth)*
Salles, Walter
   1998—*Central do Brasil (Central Station)*

Index

Page numbers for illustrations appear in *italics*.

coco, ix, 95, 144n3 (chap. 1)

coco de embolada, ix

Coco Irmãs Lopes, 23, 57, 59, 60, 122

Coco Raízes (Samba de Coco Raízes de Arcoverde): alliances in music industry, 104–8; ambitions of, 19; at Arcoverde São João Festival, 39–40, 80–82, *82*, 90–91; autoconstruction and, xv; at Carnaval, Recife (2004), 40–42; Chamber of Commerce fair and, 42; Ciço's departure from, 114, 121; cultural identity and, 71; departures from tradition, 35; *ensaios* (rehearsals), 92–94; European tour and international CD distribution, 105, 108; first CD, recording and production of, 35–39; formation of, 9–10; *Globo Comunidade* documentary and, 59; as "group" rather than "band," 35; and heritage versus professionalization, 39; after Lula's death, x; nostalgia unsettled by, xiii–xiv; and participatory versus presentation form, 43; relationship with Cordel, 57, 69, 139; as representative traditional group, 91; shopping mall fashion show and, 42–43; transition between house, street, and stage, 11

Coco Trupé de Arcoverde, 122

collaborations, international, 108, 147n10

Conselheiro, Antonio, 45, 48, 54, 125

"Construção" (Buarque), 87

Cordel do Fogo Encantado: about, xi–xii; Arcoverde, Lirinha on citation of, 111; at Arcoverde São João Festival, 83–85, *84*, *85*, 90; at Bar do Zaca, 8–9; Brazilian cinema and, 51–54; with Calixto family, 19; cultural rescue and, 14–15, 16, 70–71; death metal, MPB, and, 46–51; end of, 130–32; final São João performance (2009), 119–21; first performance at SESC, 13–15; formation of, xi; genre and tradition, engagement with, 34–35; literature, poetry, and, 54–56; *mangue beat* and, xi, 44–46, 47–49; music videos, 65–70; nostalgia unsettled by, xiii–xiv; *O Palhaço do Circo Sem Futuro*, 67; at Pan-American Games (2007), 115–16; Recife phase of, 15–19; in São Paulo, 56–57, 109; relationship with Coco Raízes, 57, 69, 139; sound effect sources for, 109–10; tour with, 122–28; as tourist inspiration, 68. *See also* Lirinha (José Paes de Lira Filho)

"O Cordel Estradeiro," 13–14, 17–18, 144n7 (chap. 1)

Cruzeiro do Nordeste, 101–2

cultural rescue (*resgate*): Cordel and, 14–15, 16, 70–71; Lirinha on, 128–29; as point of contention, xii–xiii

cultura popular (folk or traditional culture), 70

culture, "making" (*fazendo cultura*), 26, 32, 33, 34, 136

culture bearer role: Cordel and, 14, 15, 46; Cordel members and, 132; ethnography and, xx; strictures of being marked as, 115; visitor encounters and, xvi, 94, 95

Cunha, Euclides da, 125

Da lama ao caos (From mud to chaos) (Chico Science), 44

dancing: Coco Raízes performances, 40; Coco Raízes and standardization of, 43; *parcela* and *trupé* steps, 40, 94–95; steps and patterns of *samba de coco*, 11–12; *trupé* dance contests, 95; *trupé* as idealization, 136

death metal, 46–51

Dent, Alexander S., 145n3 (chap. 3)

descaracterização, 111–12

Deus e o Diabo na Terra do Sol (Black God, White Devil) (film), 53

DJ Dolores, 35, 43

"Dos três mal-amados," 55

"drinking from the wellspring" (*bebendo da fonte*), 69, 70, 72, 73

ecstatic religion, 19, 48, 55

Enrique, Nego, 16, 123, 131, 132

Entranced Earth (*Terra em Transe*) (film), 53

ethnography, xix–xx

ethnomusicological tourism, 96

exclusion and inclusion, idiosyncratic play of, xvii. *See also* citizenship; class hierarchies and mobility

family feud, Calixto-Lopes, 20–24, 29–30, 59. *See also* museums

fashion show at Paço Alfandega, 42–43

favelas (shantytowns): Arcoverde as *favela light* in the *sertão light*, xv, 72–73, 136; conflicting ideas of citizenship and, 142; high-rise fortification versus autoconstruction in, xv; Lirinha on origins of, 126–27; and the *sertão*, in Cordel and Cinema Novo, 45, 51–54, 127

fazendo cultura (making culture), 26, 32, 33, 34, 136

looping, 36
Lopes, Ivo: death of, 12; festival mud house museum in honor of, 77; history of *samba de coco* and, 12; photographs of, 27, 29, 60; Wilson on, 130
Lopes, Josefa, 24
Lopes, Lení, 24, 25, 59, 115
Lopes, Severina: in *Central Station*, 54; Coco da Irmãs Lopes, creation of, 23; in *Globo Comunidade* documentary, 60; Ivo Lopes Museum and, 24–30; Lopes-Calixto split and, 20–21, 29–30; at Lula Calixto's funeral, 20–21
Lopes family: efforts to revive status of, 139; before family feud, 12; family feud with Calixtos, 21–24, 29–30; Ivo Lopes Museum, 24–30
Lula Calixto Cultural Space (museum), x, 6, 30–31, *31*, 32
Lula da Silva, Luiz Inácio, 116, 123, 128
Luz, Zé da, 56

MacCannell, Dean, 93
mangue beat: Cordel and, xi, 44–46, 47–49; defined, xi–xii; Emerson Calado on, 131–32; founding of, 44; intertextual gaps and, xvii; Potter on, 105
"mangue jazz," 105
marionette figures at São João Festival, 118–19, *120*
Marley, Bob, 30, 140
Marques, Ana Claudia, 23–24
Marsalis, Branford, 105–7
"A Matadeira (Ou no balanço da justiça)," 123–27
Matta, Roberto da, viii
"O Medroso," 108
"Memória," 134–35
Mestre Ambrósio, 96, 107–8
Minha Cidade, Minha Saudades (Wilson), 129–30
Mission of Folkloric Research, vii, ix, xvii, 4
modernity: Cascudo on tradition and, 4–5; *Globo Comunidade* documentary and, 62; Irã Calixto and, 62; Lirinha on *descaracterização* and, 111–12; margins of, 88; partial erasure of, 90; stability of cultural transmission and, 71
Mossoró, 123
Moura, Helton, xix, 9, 97, 98, 112
Movimento Armorial, 15
MTV videos, 65–70
mud huts (*casas de taipa*), 77, *78*, 89, 99–104, 117

Mundo Livre S/A, 44
museums: as cabinets of curiosities, 31–33; Ivo Lopes Museum, 24–30, *26*, *27*, 32; Lula Calixto Cultural Space, x, 6, 30–31, *31*, 32; mud house museum at São João Festival, Arcoverde, 77, *78*, 89; split and family feud, 20–24
música caipira, 50
música de raíz (roots music), xvii, 8, 44, 134
Música Popular Brasileira (MPB), xiii, 46–47
música regional (regional music), xvii, 110
mutationism and traditionalism, 19, 46, 132, 138, 140, 145n3 (chap. 3)

Nabuco, Joaquim, viii
Nagib, Lúcia, 69
Nascimento, Milton, 46–47, 49–50
"Na veia" (song and video), 65–68, 70
Neguinho, Biu, 10, 12, 107, 147n9
Neiva, Amélia, 9–10, 22, 137
Neiva, Suedson, 9–10, 56, 118
neoliberalism and expansion of citizenship, 136–42
New Orleans, 106, 116
nostalgia (*saudade*): Cascudo on, 4–5; citizenship in the postauthoritarian moment and, 137–42; fortification versus autoconstruction and, xv; *Globo Comunidade* documentary and, 63–65; Ivo Lopes Museum and, 24–29; in music videos, 67–68; Potter and, 107; restorative versus reflective, xiii–xiv, 137; *samba de coco* as embodiment of premodern cultural memory, 88; *samba de coco* heritage and, 12; São João Festival and, 64; *saudade* as, viii; slavery legacy and, 64; spatial and temporal distancing, 71, 90; the uncanny and, 141; Wilson's *Minha Cidade, Minha Saudades*, 129–30
novenário, 27–28

Paço Alfandega shopping mall, 42–43
Padilha, Alberone, xix, 8–9, 112
O palhaço degolado (The beheaded clown) (film), 146n3 (chap. 5)
O Palhaço do Circo Sem Futuro (Cordel), 67
Palmares, Zumbi dos, 44–45
Pan-American Games (2007), 115–16
pandeiro, x
parcela steps, 40, 94, 95
Partido dos Trabalhadores, 128
Pastor (singer of Cobaias), 85–87, 114–15
pastoril, 146n2 (chap. 5)

MUSIC / CULTURE
A series from Wesleyan University Press
Edited by Deborah Wong, Sherrie Tucker, and Jeremy Wallach

Originating editors: George Lipsitz, Susan McClary, and Robert Walser

ABOUT THE AUTHOR

Daniel B. Sharp is an assistant professor at Tulane University, jointly appointed in music and Latin American studies. His articles have appeared in *Latin American Music Review*, *Brazilian Popular Music and Citizenship*, and *Critical Studies in Improvisation*.